Disunion within the Union

Ukrainian Research Institute
Harvard University

Harvard Papers in Ukrainian Studies

HURI Editorial Board

Michael S. Flier
George G. Grabowicz
Serhii Plokhy, *Chairman*

Oleh Kotsyuba, *Manager of Publications*

Cambridge, Massachusetts

Disunion within the Union

The Uniate Church and the Partitions of Poland

Distributed by Harvard University Press
for the Ukrainian Research Institute
Harvard University

The Harvard Ukrainian Research Institute was established in 1973 as an integral part of Harvard University. It supports research associates and visiting scholars who are engaged in projects concerned with all aspects of Ukrainian studies. The Institute also works in close cooperation with the Committee on Ukrainian Studies, which supervises and coordinates the teaching of Ukrainian history, language, and literature at Harvard University.

Publication of this book has been made possible in part by the generous support of Ukrainian studies at Harvard University by Dr. Ivan Kindrat and Family Fund.

ISBN 9780674246287 (paper), 9780674246393 (epub), 9780674246409 (Kindle), 9780674246416 (PDF)

Library of Congress Control Number: 2019952668
LC record available at https://lccn.loc.gov/2019952668

Cover illustration: Drawings of St. George Cathedral in Lviv, Ukraine.
Cover by Mykola Leonovych.

Contents

Note on Transliteration

Transliteration follows Library of Congress romanization rules without the use of ligatures. Toponyms are given in the language of the current jurisdiction, without primes except in the case of *Rus´*. Names of long standing in English (e.g., Warsaw) are given in that form. The capital city of Ukraine is given as Kyiv. For much of the period covered in this book, Ukrainian, Belarusian, Polish, and Lithuanian figures were active in a shared social, intellectual, and religious milieu. Since this publication selects authors and works important to the Ukrainian part of this sphere, most names are transliterated here, with primes, in their modern Ukrainian forms.

Preface

The publication of this study of the Uniate Church in the eighteenth century takes me back to the very beginnings of my academic life. It was a study that was originally suggested—indeed, commissioned—by the late Omeljan Pritsak. He was my undergraduate professor at Harvard in the 1970s and knew me from the very young age of eighteen, when I first set foot in his office at the Ukrainian Research Institute, Harvard University (HURI), at 1583 Massachusetts Avenue. It was he who introduced me to the history of Eastern Europe during that decade of HURI's founding, and I was present for his inaugural lecture ("The Origins of Rus´") as Harvard's first Mykhailo Hrushevs´kyi Professor of Ukrainian History. I think it must have been in his office at HURI that for the first time in my life I heard about the Uniate Church and began to understand its particular religious and historical significance.

Professor Pritsak was immensely generous in making time for me, a clueless undergraduate with an interest in the history of Eastern Europe, and we discussed a very wide variety of historical readings and issues, with me asking naïve questions and him answering with the full and dazzling range of his erudition.

It was in the 1980s, when I finished my PhD at Stanford, that Professor Pritsak invited me to prepare an essay on the Uniates as part of a broadly conceived intellectual project in anticipation of the millennium of Rus´ Christianity in 1988. I had just finished a doctoral dissertation on the Vatican and Poland in the age of the partitions (which appeared as a monograph in that same millennial year), addressing a range of ecclesiastical and political issues including the fate of the Uniate Church in the altered international context.

While I published an article on the Uniates in *Harvard Ukrainian Studies* in 1984, the larger project of studies on Rus´ Christianity, including my own, finally appeared in the journal in 2007, almost twenty years after the Rus´ Christian millennium. My original draft was focused especially on episcopal perspectives on the religious and political questions of the age, reflecting my research on Poland and the Vatican, but I began to think more carefully during the 1990s about issues of religious identity and the practices of piety in early modern Europe. While great scholars like Natalie Zemon Davis had pioneered an exceptionally nuanced approach to issues of piety in France, such work was rarer for the Eastern European context, and I was particularly struck by the subtlety of David Frick's approach to the issues of religious identity between Orthodoxy and the Union in the seventeenth century, in a monograph about Meletii Smotryts´kyi published by HURI in 1995.[1] When I returned to revise my own work on the Uniates, I wanted to bring these issues of piety together with the problems of ecclesiastical politics, yielding the structure of the current study: the first part focused on Church and state, and the second part on ritual and identity.

In the years since the first version of this study appeared in *Harvard Ukrainian Studies*, important research has been published on the subject, and I have tried to take this new work into account in preparing this revised version for publication. I have

---

1   Frick, David A., *Meletij Smotryc´kyj* (Cambridge, Mass.: HURI, 1995).

been gratified to see that the arguments I originally presented can be largely sustained in light of new research, and have perhaps even shaped the way some of that new research has been presented. In 2009, Barbara Skinner published her monograph on the eighteenth-century Uniates (*The Western Front of the Eastern Church*), which frames her comprehensive research from the Russian archives, and in 2012, Richard Butterwick published his landmark study of the Four-Year Sejm (*The Polish Revolution and the Catholic Church*), which offers meticulous research from the Polish archives. Some of Skinner's research appeared in *Slavic Review* in 2005, while Butterwick's article "Deconfessionalization," focusing on Ruthenia, appeared in *Central Europe* in 2008. Also immensely stimulating for me in rethinking this study has been David Frick's pioneering 2013 study of religious life in seventeenth-century Vilnius (*Kith, Kin, and Neighbors*), which considers the coexistence of religious confessions, including the Uniates, in that city; additionally, Paschalis Kitromilides's research on eighteenth-century Greek history has been indispensable for my understanding of the wider Orthodox world, especially the book published in 2013 under the title *Enlightenment and Revolution*. I also note Andrei Zorin's important book on literature and state ideology in Russia (including, notably, the era of Catherine's Russia), which appeared in Russian in 2001 and then in English translation as *By Fables Alone*, in 2014.

My perspective on the Uniates in Galicia has evolved during the last decade as I carried out the research for my own book, *The Idea of Galicia*, published in 2010. As before, I remain indebted to the pathbreaking books on the Uniates that were published in the 1990s by John-Paul Himka (*Religion and Nationality in Western Ukraine*, a study of nineteenth-century Galicia) and Borys Gudziak (*Crisis and Reform*, a study of the Union of 1596). I am confident that ongoing research projects on the Uniates by young scholars will further transform the scholarly dimensions of this subject over the course of the next generation.[2]

---

2   See Larry Wolff, "The Uniate Church and the Partitions of Poland: Religious Survival in an Age of Enlightened Absolutism," *Harvard Ukrainian Studies* 26 (2002/3): 153-244; Barbara Skinner, *The Western Front of the Eastern Church: Uniate and Orthodox Conflict in 18th-Century Poland, Ukraine, Belarus, and Russia* (DeKalb: Northern Illinois UP, 2009); Barbara Skinner, "Borderlands of Faith: Reconsidering the Origins of a Ukrainian Tragedy," *Slavic Review* 64, no. 1 (Spring 2005): 88-116; Richard Butterwick, *The Polish Revolution and the Catholic Church, 1788-1792: A Political History* (Oxford: Oxford UP, 2012); Butterwick, "Deconfessionalization: The Policy of the Polish Revolution toward Ruthenia, 1788-1792," *Central Europe* 6, no. 2 (2008): 91-121; David Frick, *Kith, Kin, and Neighbors: Communities and Confessions in Seventeenth-Century Wilno* (Ithaca: Cornell UP, 2013); Paschalis Kitromilides, *Enlightenment and Revolution: The Making of Modern Greece* (Cambridge: Harvard UP, 2013); Andrei Zorin, *By Fables Alone: Literature and State Ideology in Late-Eighteenth-Early-Nineteenth-Century Russia*, trans. Marcus Levitt (2001; Boston: Academic Studies Press, 2014); Larry Wolff, *The Idea of Galicia: History and Fantasy in Habsburg Political Culture* (Stanford: Stanford UP, 2010); Borys Gudziak, *Crisis and Reform: The Kyivan Metropolitanate, the Patriarch of Constantinople, and the Genesis of the Union of Brest* (Cambridge, Mass.: HURI, 1998); John-Paul Himka, *Religion and Nationality in Western Ukraine: The Greek Catholic Church and the Ruthenian National Movement in Galicia, 1867-1900* (Montreal: McGill-Queen's UP, 1999).

Introduction: *Disunion within the Union*

"We are experiencing disunion within the Union itself," observed
Iason Smohozhevs´kyi (Jason Smogorzewski), the Uniate archbishop of Polatsk (Polack, Połock), in May 1774. "The body of
the Uniates is split into so many completely different parts, and
subject to diverse heads."[3] In fact, the aspects of disunion were
manifold. Principally, there was the very recent shock of the
first partition of Poland in 1772, which transformed the Union all
at once from a religious phenomenon of the Polish-Lithuanian
Commonwealth to an international Church in the Russian and
Habsburg empires, as well as in the remains of the Commonwealth. The Uniates were now subject to the "crowned heads" of
Catherine, Maria Theresa, Joseph, and Stanisław August. At the
same time, the lines of ecclesiastical authority within the Uniate
Church were "split," as the demarcations of partition fragmented
the domain of the metropolitanate without corresponding to
the diocesan boundaries. Smohozhevs´kyi was now a subject
of Catherine II and already knew he was cut off from the authority of the metropolitan across the border in Poland. When
Smohozhevs´kyi himself became metropolitan in the 1780s and

---

3   Jason Smogorzewski, *Epistolae Jasonis Junosza Smogorzevskyj, metro-
politae Kioviensis Catholici, 1780–1788*, Analecta OSBM, ser. 2, sec. 3, ed. Athanasius G. Welykyj (Rome, 1965), 120. All translations are my own.

left Russia behind him, he was similarly severed from his former diocese of Polatsk. In 1774, however, there was also disunion within the Uniate hierarchy (as Smohozhevsʹkyi well knew, for he had vainly attempted to mediate), and disputes of episcopal authority among the bishops had reached such a crisis that they raided each other's ecclesiastical properties while posting furious accusations and counteraccusations to the Vatican. Although that divisive struggle was, to a certain extent, the product of specific personalities and circumstances, there was nothing accidental about the mounting fundamental tensions between the privileged and prosperous Basilian order of Uniate monks and the downtrodden secular clergy who attended to the parish flocks. All these factors of "disunion within the Union" were especially debilitating at a time when the Uniates faced the gravest external pressures as well: the nationalizing pressure of enlightened states and the proselytizing pressure of rival religions.

Smohozhevsʹkyi carried himself very carefully in May 1774, and, right after noting the problem of "diverse heads," he recorded the celebration of Catherine's birthday (2 May) in his own Church, followed by a dinner in his own home. That same first week of May ended with the festival of St. Stanisław, which the archbishop also celebrated until midnight in honor of his patron and former sovereign, the king of Poland. He obtained Russian official permission for this party, and, hoping that no one would be offended by his marking of the occasion, he included important local Russians on the guest list. When Smohozhevsʹkyi remarked upon the splitting of the "body of the Uniates" he was probably conscious of the implied analogy between the religious body of his Church and the political body of partitioned Poland. Throughout the last quarter of the eighteenth century their fates would obviously be analogous and, at the same time, quite subtly interrelated. The Uniate archbishop, who had just the week before celebrated the festival of a Roman Catholic saint in an Orthodox state, could have contemplated the political implications of the eleventh-century martyrdom of St. Stanisław—his body dismembered and then miraculously recomposed. Yet, if Smohozhevs´kyi meditated on miracles, he was nevertheless an ecclesiastical statesman fully attuned to the pragmatic implications of worldly politics for religious affairs. First as archbishop of Polatsk under Russian rule after 1772, and then as the Uniate metropolitan in the Commonwealth from 1779 until his death in 1788, Smohozhevs´kyi confronted perhaps more directly and comprehensively than any other Uniate leader the changing political and episcopal circumstances that followed the first partition of Poland. His perspective on Uniate disunion will serve as the focus for this analysis of the Uniate Church in the age of the Polish partitions.

The last quarter of the eighteenth century constitutes an historically coherent period in the history of the Uniate Church. This periodization rests on the chronological framework of the Polish partitions, for it was the dramatic international and political changes of 1772, 1793, and 1795 that conditioned the cultural and religious crisis of the Uniates. The founding of the Uniate Church at the Union of Brest of 1596 occurred under the sovereignty and sponsorship of the Commonwealth; the period from Poland's humiliation in 1772 to Poland's elimination in 1795 witnessed the weaning of the Uniates from their fundamentally Polish political framework and, ultimately, the cutting of their connection to the Commonwealth. At the same time this was the age of the French Revolution in which the ancien régime of early modern Europe faced the rumblings of modernity, and the Uniate Church was no exception in its experience of transitional development at this historical juncture. The crucial period of transition from the early modern establishment of the Union in the Polish-Lithuanian Commonwealth to the modern national development of the Uniates in Ukraine occurred in the late eighteenth century, the age of the Polish partitions.

The Uniate Church was dramatically affected by the unprecedented instability of political geography caused by the partitions, as territories changed sovereignty according to the diplomatic negotiations of the partitioning powers. The Uniate

Church measured its fragmentation in episcopal dioceses, and already in 1772 those of Lviv and Przemyśl (Peremyshl) were of the portion assigned to Austria, whereas the archbishopric of Polatsk lay in the lands of Belarus claimed by Catherine II. The division of the Church among three different sovereignties—Austrian, Russian, and Polish—was traumatic enough, since the whole history of the Uniates to that point was barely conceivable apart from the sponsorship of the Commonwealth. In 1793 and 1795, however, when the Commonwealth ceased to exist altogether, the dioceses of Volodymyr, Lutsk, Chełm (Kholm), Kam'ianets, Pinsk, and Brest, as well as the metropolitan diocese of Ukraine, found themselves in either Russia or Austria—with additional bits incongruously assigned to Prussia, including the important Basilian monastery at Supraśl.

This unstable geopolitical base created serious problems of ecclesiastical adaptation, but in fact the partitioners' appropriation of dioceses was the most straightforward aspect of the Uniate circumstances. Changing sovereignties brought with it radically disruptive eighteenth-century intrusions of state upon Church, in both Austria and Russia, while the whole period was also punctuated by intervals of potent pressure at the parish level to leave the Union altogether. These disturbances occurred not only in the newly annexed lands of Orthodox Russia, but also in Poland, where Catherine II retained a dominant influence after 1772. At the close of each interval, however, when pressure to apostatize was lifted, there was a return to the fold of the Union. In addition to this periodic ebb and flow between Orthodoxy and Union, there were also those Uniates who chose to escape that alternative by anchoring themselves somewhat more stably in the Roman Catholic Church. The Vatican itself officially disapproved of this "transit" from the Union, but Rome's effective control over ecclesiastical activities in the relevant regions was distinctly limited. Such a high degree of religious motility on the parish level, set in the context of the diocesan rearrangements dictated by the partitions, made the Uniate Church in the late eighteenth century something virtually kaleidoscopic in its divisions, variations, and permutations.

The problems and pressures that the Uniates experienced under Russian sovereignty after 1772, as well as in Poland as a consequence of Russian influence, guaranteed that nineteenth-century Church historians would make their accounts into chronicles of persecution, forced apostasy, and martyrdom, inevitably reminding their readers of the suffering and survival of the early Christians. Edward Likowski, a professor at the Roman Catholic seminary in Poznań, wrote thus of the death of Catherine II in 1796: "The eternal Judge called her to the justice of His judgment seat so that she might account for the rivers of blood and tears that flowed during her reign from millions of Uniates, solely on account of their religious conviction."[4] Iuliian Pelesh, the rector of the Uniate seminary in Vienna and ultimately a Uniate bishop, attributed the misfortunes of the Uniates to "the hellish arts of a Catherine or a Nicholas."[5] The nineteenth-century works of Likowski and Pelesh remain important for any twenty-first-century historical study of the eighteenth-century Uniate Church, but they take for granted certain historiographical perspectives that in fact may be anachronistically inappropriate for interpreting the period in question.

The demonological reference to Catherine's "hellish arts" and "rivers of blood and tears" might be noted as hyperbolic, but more subtly problematic is Likowski's interpretation of the persecution of the Uniates as occurring "solely on account of their religious conviction," especially when taken together with Pelesh's casual conflation of the reigns and aims of Catherine II and Nicholas I. It

4   Eduard Likowski, *Geschichte des allmaeligen Verfalls der unirten ruthenischen Kirche im XVIII und XIX Jahrhundert*, trans. Apollinaris Tłoczyński, vol. 1 (Poznań, 1885), 282.

5   Julian Pelesz [Iuliian Pelesh], *Geschichte der Union der ruthenischen Kirche mit Rom*, vol. 2 (Vienna, 1881), 552; see also Himka, *Religion and Nationality in Western Ukraine*, 15, 112–14, 125–26.

is true that Tsar Nicholas finally and decisively did away with the Uniate Church in the Russian Empire in 1839, but Catherine, reigning in the eighteenth century, should not be interpreted entirely in the light of her grandson. The late eighteenth century must be taken on its own historiographical terms, and not invested anachronistically with the nineteenth-century spirit of mingled religious and nationalist motivations. For if Catherine II, with her generally irreligious inclinations, is interpreted as a Russian Orthodox crusader, then it becomes difficult to appreciate the characteristic responses of the enlightened absolutist state to the issue of religious diversity.

The historian must refrain from fitting eighteenth-century developments into a schema of tragic destiny that depends on hindsight instead of history, with Nicholas I at the end of every vista, and Stalin lurking behind him. The extraordinary resurgence of the Uniate Church in Ukraine (as the Ukrainian Greek Catholic Church) in the 1990s may serve as a cautionary tale against any unilineal or determinist perspective on Uniate history, and a re-minder that political upheaval, as in the 1790s, may have volatile religious consequences. By taking the eighteenth century on its own terms it is possible to offer a distinctive historiographical agenda with a set of interrelated arguments. First, the conse-quences of the Polish partitions for the Uniate Church did not develop as part of a grand design, but, quite the contrary, were the improvised responses, from both inside and outside the Uniate Church, to the unprecedented shock of the partitions. Second, though Catherine became the "hellish" nemesis of the Uniates, while Maria Theresa and Joseph II were hailed as its beneficent patrons and saviors, in fact the divergent Austrian and Russian approaches to the Uniate Church grew out of startlingly similar principles: the characteristic enlightened ("Josephinist") inter-vention of the state in Church affairs. Third, while hindsight may reveal Russian Orthodoxy as the mortal enemy of the Uniate Church, late eighteenth-century Uniates, even within the Rus-sian Empire, were often at least equally apprehensive about the possibly aggressive intentions of Roman Catholicism, especially as represented by the Polish episcopal hierarchy and the not-quite-suppressed Jesuit order.

Finally, one finds in the Uniate Church of the late eighteenth century not so much the utterly committed self-certainty of the early Christians who embraced their martyrdoms, but rather a profound crisis of identity that reflected the "disunion in the Union." There was religious ambivalence in every stratum within the Uniate Church—the bishops, the Basilians, the parish priests, the local laity—as well as uncertainty from without, as outsiders—Russian and Polish, Orthodox and Roman—consulted their own interests in constructing an identity for a religious community that was wrestling with the problem of identifying itself. Those intervals during which hundreds of Uniate parishes left the Union and then returned again, repeatedly leaving and reuniting in response to the pressures of the moment, made the issue of identity all the more urgent to contemporaries—and it remains similarly challenging to historians. This study seeks to outline the historical problems in their eighteenth-century dimensions, especially as perceived within the Uniate hierarchy and in correspondence with the Vatican.

"In truth," observed Smohozhevs´kyi in 1774, "all the evils and every danger now seem to be enveloped in the perplexity of that one little word: Catholics."[6] It is true that the Russian authorities did not always recognize the Uniates as Catholics, but Smohozhevs´kyi himself was often preoccupied with the "perplexity" of the Uniates' sense of their own Catholicism. Though even a bishop like Smohozhevs´kyi might be theologically ambivalent about the Uniate religious compromise between Orthodoxy and Catholicism, those at the top of the hierarchy did not hesitate to attribute the uncertain identity of the lower clergy and their flocks to a lamentable "ignorance." The problem of "ignorance" came up constantly throughout the period, along with a reiterated concern

---

6   Smogorzewski, *Epistolae*, 139.

about education. In this respect the preoccupations of the Uniate Church corresponded to those of the period in general. The call for education among the Uniates coincided and intersected with the reforms of the National Education Commission in Poland, the controversial continuation of Jesuit school education in Russia, and the Josephinist intervention in religious education in Austria. The importance of education, both secular and religious, was emphasized throughout Europe in the age of the Enlightenment. In the case of the Uniates it was seen as significant for the consolidation of religious identity. While the first part of this study will explore changing religious circumstances as an issue of relations between Church and state, the second part will focus on the relevance of ritual and identity for Uniate religious survival.

General ignorance, even among the parish clergy, constituted a less urgent problem for the Uniate Church in early modern Poland, when a reasonably stable hierarchy of dioceses and parishes was held in place by a relatively functional Polish-Lithuanian state. After 1772 the new divisions with their consequent pressures encouraged the Church to put greater emphasis on raising the religious consciousness of its parish clergy and peasant constituents. The attentions of the Uniate Church hierarchy to the proverbial *wiara chłopska* or "peasant faith" of its members would have the ultimate effect of opening up the Church's tightly circumscribed social and cultural norms, making possible a broader national and religious engagement of society in the nineteenth century.

In Rome in 1773, at the missionary congregation of the Propaganda Fide, the committee of cardinals considered the need for "concord" so that "in such dangerous times as these the Uniate Ruthenian Church may be spared the scandals and divisions that can cause it infinite harm."[7] The term "Ruthenian" was employed throughout this period to designate the Uniate Church, along

---

7   *Acta S. C. de Propaganda Fide: Ecclesiam Catholicam Ucrainae et Bielarusjae Spectantia*, vol. 5 *(1769–1862)*, Analecta OSBM, ser. 2, sec. 3, ed. Athanasius G. Welykyj (Rome, 1955), 60.

with its rituals and populations, from Belarus to Ukraine. Though the name was hardly an expression of modern nationalism, its usage assigned to the Uniates a certain cultural coherence in the face of so many imposed divisions. The hope of bringing concord out of division at this point, in 1773, seemed almost to reflect a nostalgia for the early modern political and religious order in Poland that could never again be recovered. The particular scandal under discussion was the episcopal squabbling among the Uniate bishops, but that was only one of the manifold contemporary forms of disunion threatening "infinite harm" in "dangerous times." "Concord" was perhaps beyond recovery, but in exploring its own divisions and addressing itself to the identity of its constituents, the Uniate Church in the late eighteenth century also confronted the challenges that appeared at the threshold of modern European history.

Part I. Church and State

Principles of Authority

In 1782 Tsarina Catherine II gave her Warsaw ambassador a message for Pope Pius VI, insisting that he create a Roman Catholic archbishopric in Russia for her cooperative pet bishop, Stanisław Siestrzeńcewicz. The pope was to be informed, in no uncertain terms, that if he did not swallow his objections to Siestrzeńcewicz and promptly provide the ceremonial regalia for the grand promotion, the tsarina would not hesitate to withdraw her protection from the Catholic Church in Russia. The consequences, Catherine pointed out, would be particularly grave for the Uniates who resided in the Belarusian lands detached from Poland in 1772:

> The Pope himself cannot be ignorant of the fact that most of those
> who profess the Roman communion under my government of
> White Russia were once of our Orthodox religion, and that they
> and their ancestors only adopted the Roman communion on account of the persecution they experienced in Poland and the artifices of Roman priests. Under these circumstances, the majority of
> them await only the least signal to embrace our Orthodox religion,
> which they abandoned with regret and of which they retain many
> traces and vestiges in their hearts—a religion whose dogmas are all
> the more precious to humanity inasmuch as they have never been

found in contradiction with the principles of authority and civil
power, nor with the well-being and the administration (*la police*) of
states.[8]

The tsarina's reading of Uniate history was simplistic, one-sided,
and self-serving, but not so wildly off the mark as to fail to put
across her basic point: that the balance of power in the region,
which had favored Poland and Catholicism at the time of the
Union in 1596, had now shifted decisively in favor of Russia and
Orthodoxy. For Catherine, the past history, current crisis, and
future fate of the Uniates was, above all, a question of power.
Her interest in the "traces and vestiges in their hearts" suggests
that she was attuned to the political significance of Uniate religious identity. Orthodoxy, which she claimed to see as a vestigial
feature of the Union, revealed its preciousness in its relation to
"principles of authority" and "the administration of states."

These were, of course, the great political issues of enlightened
absolutism in eighteenth-century Europe, and they were particularly sensitive in empires confronting a diversity of cultural
and religious communities. Catherine in the 1770s immediately
addressed the administrative problems raised by her acquisitions
from Poland, and remained attuned to the religious ramifications
of those problems throughout her reign. In the 1780s, the Josephine revolution in Habsburg relations between Church and state
also addressed these issues of authority and civil power. In the
1790s, at the Four-Year Sejm, the Polish-Lithuanian Commonwealth
itself reorganized its religious institutions in that spirit of state
authority and government involvement—a spirit not altogether
unrelated to that of the simultaneously codified Civil Constitution
of the Clergy in revolutionary France. Whatever the evolving
religious climates for the Uniate Church—nourishing in Austria,
harassing in Russia, ambivalent in Poland—the fundamental

---

8   Archivio della Nunziatura di Varsavia, Registro 65 (hereafter ANV 65),
"Copia tirata dal Dispaccio originale dell'Imperatrice di Russia al suo Ambasci-
atore in Varsavia," 408.

institutional engagement of Church by state was structurally similar. The terms of that engagement were defined according to the values of enlightened absolutism by the governments in Vienna, St. Petersburg, and Warsaw, pursuing analogous political agendas, however divergent the ultimate religious consequences.

Pacification

Catherine II, from the moment she cast her imperial eye on Poland in the 1760s, was inspired to present herself as the enlightened patroness of religious freedom against the alleged intolerance of the Commonwealth. Voltaire led the pack of philosophes who acclaimed her imperial policy of power as a crusade of the Enlightenment. From the very start of the reign of King Stanisław August, whose royal election Catherine arranged in 1764, an Orthodox campaign was mounted against Uniate parishes in the eastern lands of the Commonwealth, and some communities were encouraged to take an oath of Orthodoxy: "that we and our descendants shall eternally and without fail preserve the Greek-Russian faith, oppose with every means the Roman Uniate faith," or else "submit ourselves to the unforgiving last judgment and to eternal damnation."[9] With such religious polarization taking place at the village level, Catherine herself began interfering in Polish affairs with a memorandum to Warsaw favoring equal civil rights for Poland's non-Catholics, the Dissidents. This demand for legislative equality was presented to the Sejm in 1766 and formalized in an imposed Russian-Polish treaty as the religious articles of 1768.

Catherine thus gave satisfaction to her own Russian Orthodox hierarchy inasmuch as she offered protection to the Orthodox peasant population in the eastern lands of the Commonwealth. For Orthodoxy, like Protestantism, was "dissident" in Catholic Poland, and Orthodox grievances targeted not just Catholic dominance by law in the Commonwealth, but the ongoing pastoral struggle

---

9   Skinner, *Western Front*, 26.

between Orthodox and Uniates that dated back to the Union of 1596. The Uniate Church did not spring fully formed from the Union of Brest: such dioceses as Lviv and Przemyśl remained Orthodox through the seventeenth century, and during the first half of the eighteenth century the Union continued to aggrandize itself among the communities of Ukraine under the sponsorship of the Commonwealth. In the articles of 1768, Catherine determined to set back this ongoing displacement of Orthodoxy by the Union, and a tribunal was proposed to settle disputes with reference to the status quo of a hundred years before. Political explosions forestalled such a resolution at that time, but Catherine had already elaborated the perspective that would lead her to later denounce the Uniates for "persecution" of the Orthodox.

The mounting tensions of the 1760s finally erupted into warfare in 1768 when Catherine's treaty articles on behalf of the Dissidents provoked patriotic Catholic Poles to take up arms in the Confederation of Bar, and to fight against their own king and his Russian patroness. For Catherine, this quickly turned into a two-front war against the Ottoman Empire as well as the Polish Confederation. Ukraine, the heartland of the Uniate Church, constituted the intermediary terrain between Turkey and Poland, and was overrun by Russian troops. This Russian military presence in the lands of the Commonwealth created a domain in which Warsaw could not hope to govern or protect its subjects. At the same time, an Orthodox missionary crusade against the Uniate parishes of Ukraine was unleashed from beyond the Dnieper River, led by the bishop of Pereiaslav, while a campaign of insurrectionary violence was directed against Roman Catholics, Uniates, and Jews, led by Haidamak Cossack bands. This latter violence culminated in the Uman massacre, in which the Haidamaks seized the Uniate Basilian monks and "paraded them naked and barely alive amidst abuses and sneers around the town hall" before murdering them. The Basilian Uniate church in Uman was desecrated by the Orthodox insurrectionaries, who were reported to have "dashed the ciborium with the holy sacrament to the ground, trampled on the image of the Savior on the cross, speared it with pikes, shot it through, and finally hung it by the head."[10] The conventions of sacrilege clearly did not apply in the fiercely antagonistic climate of Orthodox-Uniate conflict. Catherine felt obliged to dissociate herself and her state from such irregular atrocities, but the ravages of the Haidamaks certainly helped to create a convenient political void and chaos in those strategic lands which she intended to occupy for the duration of hostilities.

With Russian troops negating the efficacy of Polish government in Ukraine, and Haidamak bands adding an element of terror, the Orthodox missionary effort met with great success. Uniate priests were pressured to convert to Orthodoxy and bring their parishes with them, while those who resisted were expelled and replaced. Thus began a period of intense pressure on the Uniate Church which did not abate until after the partition of 1772, and did not cease completely until the treaty settlement of 1775. During this period, more than a thousand Uniate parishes in Ukraine were taken over by Orthodox priests. Missionaries, however, did not achieve these impressive results entirely on their own; Russian soldiers actively collaborated in the crusade. At Bila Tserkva, for instance, the Orthodox priest Vasyl´ Zrazhevs´kyi and the Russian captain Kruglov worked together to arrest all the local Uniate priests on Christmas Eve, keeping them locked up through Christmas Day.[11] Such local teamwork reflected the presumed collaboration at the highest level between Hervazii Lyntsevs´kyi, the Orthodox bishop of Pereiaslav, and General Piotr Rumiantsev, the Russian commander in Ukraine. Catherine formalized the religious role of her army in Ukraine with an ukaz of 1771 that authorized the protection of Orthodox communities from Uniate persecution. Thus, she continued to present herself as the champion of religious freedom.

---

10   Skinner, *Western Front*, 132–33.

11   Pelesz, *Geschichte der Union*, 2:561.

Regardless of who was actually the object of persecution (by 1771, the balance already had shifted against the Uniates), the point of the ukaz was to express Catherine's official approval of the arbitration and interference of her military officials (indeed, mandating it). In 1768, she had involved herself in Polish religious affairs by bilateral treaty; now she did so by unilateral decree. In fact, in 1771 it was almost meaningless to speak of Poland's sovereignty in Ukraine: the war was ongoing, and the partition was under negotiation. Under these circumstances, for the duration of the war, Catherine could issue decrees against Uniate persecution; her soldiers could arrest Uniate priests; and her missionaries could take over Uniate parishes. In the region around Uman, the site of the Haidamak massacre, Russian military instructions specified that the keys to village churches should be taken from Uniate priests and handed over to Orthodox priests, for "as there had formerly been the Orthodox faith, so shall there be until the end of time." With such fiercely charged crusading ideology, the religious tensions on the ground readily became violent; for instance, one Uniate priest reported that the Russian soldiers "beat me with the butts of their rifles and clubs" as the Orthodox priest took over the parish.[12] The Warsaw nuncio, Giuseppe Garampi, was trying to keep a careful account of the lost parishes, but recognized in 1772 that it would be impossible to think about restitution until after the "pacification" of Poland.[13] The religious crisis of the Uniate Church in Ukraine between 1768 and 1772 accompanied Catherine's Polish policy, from the war against the Confederation of Bar to the diplomacy of the partition settlement.

While the massacre of Uman became a byword for anti-Catholic terror in Ukraine, it was above all the imprisonment at Berdy-

---

12   Skinner, *Western Front*, 136–37.

13   Larry Wolff, "Vatican Diplomacy and the Uniates of Ukraine after the First Partition of the Polish-Lithuanian Commonwealth," *Harvard Ukrainian Studies* 8, no. 3–4 (December 1984): 404; ANV 57, Garampi, 5 December 1772.

chiv that came to epitomize the violent persecution of the Uniate Church by the Russian army. There, in 1772 and 1773, sixty-eight Uniate priests were jailed, and in 1774 the Uniate bishop of Chełm, Maksymiliian Ryllo, who was traveling throughout Ukraine to visit ecclesiastical prisoners, was himself imprisoned at Berdychiv. The case of the sixty-eight priests received considerable attention, with reports reaching Garampi at the Warsaw nunciature that the prisoners were chained, starved, and confined together in a suffocatingly inadequate space; the affair was publicized in the manner of the Black Hole of Calcutta almost twenty years before. The nuncio appealed to King Stanisław August and to Empress Maria Theresa in Vienna, while sending the prisoners copies of St. Cyprian's *Exhortation to Martyrdom*. The Uniate metropolitan sent a Polish translation for those captive priests who could not read the *Exhortation* in Latin, since they were not, after all, Roman Catholics.[14]

Martyrdom, however, was not the ultimate outcome. The priests were liberated in September 1773 at the recommendation of the Russian ambassador in Warsaw, Otto Magnus Stackelberg, and just after the ratification of the treaties of partition by the Polish Sejm. Clearly, the prisoners were not destined to follow the exhortation of St. Cyprian; the timing of their liberation revealed that all along they had been not martyrs, but hostages—hostages to Catherine's Polish policy. Once the partitions had been ratified in Warsaw, Russia could begin to relax its grip on Ukraine. As for the bishop detained in 1774, he woke up two months later to discover that his guards had disappeared and that he was free to go. In fact, the Russian government denied that he had ever been detained, dismissing the incident as "merely a Uniate calumny."[15] The years since 1768 had been years of lawless bullying

---

14   Likowski, *Geschichte des allmaeligen Verfalls*, 1:159; Sophia Senyk, "The Education of the Secular Clergy in the Ruthenian Church before the Nineteenth Century," *Orientalia Christiana Periodica* 53 (1987): 414.

15   Wolff, "Vatican Diplomacy and the Uniates," 409; ANV 58, Garampi, 23

in Ukraine, which remained in a state of suspended irregularity while Catherine fought her wars and negotiated the partition. By 1774, however, Catherine was ready to reconsider the value of social stability over irregular violence.

When the captive priests of Berdychiv were liberated in 1773, they were not restored to their parishes, which remained in the hands of the Orthodox. In this sense, the liberation, though naturally a joyous occasion, was no great institutional triumph for the Uniate Church; the thousand lost parishes remained lost, for the moment. Garampi, the nuncio, was well aware of this, and in 1774 he so despaired of not being able to influence Ukraine from Warsaw that he resorted to an extravagantly roundabout approach to the problem. From Warsaw, he urged the Vatican in Rome to appeal to Versailles so that the French king might in turn appeal to the sultan in Constantinople on behalf of the Uniates of Ukraine. Garampi hoped that the restitution of the Uniate parishes might become one of the concerns of the Ottoman Empire in its war against Russia. This peculiarly indirect and rather unlikely appeal was never properly launched, as Russia finally won the war in 1774, putting Turkey in no position to realize any desiderata at all.[16] The scheme clearly indicated, however, Garampi's sense of the urgency regarding the Uniate situation, and also suggested the apparent futility of strategies for achieving a remedy.

When the Partition Sejm in Warsaw finally concluded its two-year session in 1775 with a general confirmation of the religious articles of 1768 on behalf of the Dissidents, the question of the parishes of Ukraine was referred to a future joint commission composed of Polish and Russian members. The commission was to consider "the grievances of the Greek non-Uniates against the Greek Uniates and reciprocally of the latter against the former," phrasing that reflected Catherine's preferred emphasis on the Uniates as persecutors; it suggested that the commission would

---

July 1774.

16   Wolff, "Vatican Diplomacy and the Uniates," 414–15.

be concerned, principally, with Orthodox grievances against the Uniates, whereas the possibility of Uniate grievances was merely noted afterwards, in perfunctory fashion, as occurring "reciprocally."[17]

The commission, however, was never constituted, for by the end of 1775 the usurped parishes had suddenly begun returning to the Union. Orthodox priests were set aside, while Uniate priests who had accepted Orthodoxy under pressure now renounced their apostasy. By 1774, Ryllo, the visiting bishop, was already absolving Uniate priests of their coerced apostasies—but Ryllo was arrested at that time. Now, in 1775, the Uniates returned to the Union without obstruction, and what had seemed to promise the elimination of the Union in Ukraine was revealed as temporary harassment.

Not only the priests at Berdychiv, but their parishes, too, had been held hostage pending the "pacification" and establishment of a new order in Poland. The timing was, again, unmistakable: just as the liberation of the priests followed immediately after the ratification of the partition treaties, the return of the parishes, too, began within months of the conclusion of the Partition Sejm in Warsaw. Catherine relaxed her grip, the army ceased intervening, and the Orthodox ecclesiastical intruders lost the ability to hold on to the parishes they had acquired. Now it was Polish authorities (rather than Russian soldiers) who facilitated the changeover in these parishes, bringing about the return of Uniate priests.[18] Catherine's influence in Poland remained paramount, but now she looked on with seeming nonchalance as the parishes of Ukraine slipped back into the Union. For Catherine, the Union in Ukraine had served as a convenient pressure point in the campaign to dominate Poland, but she was not at this time committed to the elimination of the Uniates.

---

17   Wolff, "Vatican Diplomacy and the Uniates," 416; ANV 59, Garampi, 15 February 1775.

18   Skinner, *Western Front*, 171–72.

The Mutation of Temporal Dominion

The person who was most acutely aware of the political significance of religion in Ukraine during these years was the Warsaw
nuncio Garampi. When he came to Warsaw from Rome in 1772, it
seemed shocking to him that such a successful Orthodox campaign
could be mounted in the lands of the Catholic Commonwealth.
Unable at first to believe that Warsaw was really so powerless to
resist, he tried to impress upon the king, his ministers, and the
representatives at the Partition Sejm the political importance of
the Uniates for Poland. In 1773, he wrote and began to circulate
anonymously a pamphlet entitled *Exposé of the Condition of the
Church in Ukraine*. In it he appealed on behalf of the persecuted
priests, but he also pursued a carefully reasoned political analysis of what that persecution implied. Because the peasants of
Ukraine were "ignorant," Garampi feared they were "incapable of
distinguishing civil from religious obedience." Therefore, he reasoned, "when such a people is won for the Greek Oriental religion,
they will confuse the center of their religious state, which will be
St. Petersburg, with that of their political existence, which is the
Republic of Poland." Garampi, beginning to accept that Poland was
either powerless or indifferent, developed the same argument in
his 1774 suggestions for an appeal to Constantinople, insisting that
"beyond religious considerations there are political ones which
ought to interest that court." If the Uniates of Ukraine became
Orthodox, they would become assets for Russian policy against
Turkey. "Although Russia does not care at all about leaving to the
Republic of Poland dominion and sovereignty over the territory
of Ukraine," wrote Garampi, "the inhabitants nonetheless will
be, if necessary, like subjects, even more than subjects, of the
Muscovite monarchy."[19] This whole analysis of "distinguishing
civil from religious obedience," and of relating sovereignty and
subjects, was both sophisticated and prescient—perhaps too much

---

19   Skinner, *Western Front*, 412; ANV 58, Garampi, 16 July 1774.

so for the members of the Sejm. When Garampi was lobbying for a formal Polish guarantee of the rights of the Uniates in Poland, the representatives were "dazed and dead tired"—too tired to act on the nuncio's recommendation.[20]

If the Vatican was disappointed in the inaction of the Polish Sejm, the Uniate Church itself might have been less surprised. The history of the Union in the Commonwealth had always been marked by the disconcerting official concession of preeminence to Roman Catholicism—symbolized, on the highest level, by the exclusion of the Uniate bishops from the Senate. Given this historical imbalance, there was a certain irony in securing the fate of the Uniates separated from Poland with guarantees of the status quo for Catholicism "of both rites" in its aspects "both material and spiritual." Russia and Austria both agreed to this in the 1773 treaties of partition with Poland, and both states, in their respectively acquired territories of Belarus and Galicia, treated these guarantees of the status quo rather casually. (The territory annexed by Catherine in 1772, designated as White Russia or Belarus, corresponds to just the eastern part of today's Belarus.) "In the manifesto proclaiming the annexation of Belarus, Catherine had undertaken to respect the religion of its inhabitants, and in the treaty with Poland of September 1773, she bound herself to maintain the status quo with regard to the Catholic religion," wrote the historian Isabel de Madariaga. "But the Russian tradition," Madariaga continued, "by now well established, of domination over the Church signified that Catherine would interpret the status quo in her own way, namely the exclusion of any independent external (or internal) control of ecclesiastical institutions."[21] Emperor Joseph II in Habsburg Galicia would be no more respectful of the religious status quo than Catherine II in Belarus.

---

20   Wolff, "Vatican Diplomacy and the Uniates," 417; ANV 59, Garampi, 22 March 1775.

21   Likowski, *Geschichte des allmaeligen Verfalls*, 1:186; Isabel de Madariaga, *Russia in the Age of Catherine the Great* (New Haven, 1981), 512.

From the point of view of the Vatican, there was all the difference in the world between Poland losing its Uniates to Catholic Austria and to Orthodox Russia, but from within the Uniate
Church, both changes of sovereignty were greeted with tactful
expressions of confidence and optimism. In 1774 Maria Theresa's
establishment of the Uniate "Barbaraeum" seminary in Vienna
was hailed as a magnificent gesture, especially in comparison
to Poland's past indifference. In 1773 Smohozhevs´kyi in Belarus
found that the Russian authorities were "no longer complicit in
the improprieties of their priests," and that, "on the contrary,
frequenting the Catholic churches, they exhort me to the better
education of my clergy." He praised Count Zakhar Chernyshev, the
provincial governor, for his "optimal probity" and "special gentili-
ty." Smohozhevs´kyi even found the Russian generals with whom
he dealt to be "courteous, reasonable, impartial, and supremely
prudent." Catherine herself was "the most beautiful example of
goodness, clemency, and justice," not to mention "so enlightened,
so benign, and completely impartial." Was Smohozhevs´kyi really
so confident about the beneficence of Russian sovereignty, or
did he imagine that the Russian authorities might be opening
his letters? He addressed his conclusions to Pope Clement XIV
himself: "From all this Your Holiness will deign to gather that the
Catholic religion, thus succored, cannot suffer here at all from
the mutation of temporal dominion."[22] Smohozhevs´kyi would
eventually have cause to revise such optimistic first impressions.
    After 1772, while in Ukraine Russian soldiers still harassed
Uniate subjects of the Commonwealth, in Belarus the new Uniate
subjects of Catherine remained unmolested at the parish level,
and the "mutation of temporal dominion" affected the Church
only with regard to issues of high jurisdiction. In 1773, when
Smohozhevs´kyi was in St. Petersburg, he learned of the new
regulations from Chernyshev:

---

22   Smogorzewski, *Epistolae*, 108–9.

I went to visit the Count Governor in his own carriage, was honor-
ably received at the door of the company hall, and after the first
ceremonies we left the other guests and retired just the two of us
to a little cabinet where the Count confided in me that Her Imperial
Majesty would confirm me in possession of my archbishopric; that
she would not permit appeal outside the limits of her empire; that
she would not suffer in her estates any bishop who was not her
subject; and that finally every Roman communication would have
to be presented to the court before being published. To such proposals I replied with modesty that, not being an illegitimate pastor,
nor having committed any crime, I could always with the greatest
security rely upon imperial justice.[23]

Smohozhevs´kyi informed Chernyshev that if the government
wanted to regulate relations with Rome, it ought to take up the
matter with the pope.

Such innovations were greeted in the Vatican with indignant
protests about the violated status quo. In these points, however,
Catherine displayed no special malice toward the Uniates (since
Roman Catholicism in Russia was similarly regulated), and neither
did she show any great originality in her religious concerns. It
was a commonplace point of enlightened political thought that
Rome's absolute spiritual authority over its flock constituted an
infringement upon the secular authority of the absolute state.
Indeed, Joseph waited only for Maria Theresa's death in 1780 to
introduce in the Habsburg lands an even more thoroughgoing
regulation of relations between his Catholic subjects (again,
Roman and Uniate) and the Vatican. Madariaga argues that Catherine's policy involved "treating the Uniates precisely as she had
treated the Roman Catholics," and that her affirmations of state
control meant, in fact, that "the same principles which governed
the state's relations with the Orthodox Church would govern its
relations with Rome." John Alexander notes that Catherine's reign

---

23   Smogorzewski, *Epistolae*, 85.

began, in the Petrine tradition, with the arrest of the Orthodox
Metropolitan Arsenii Matsievych of the Holy Synod in 1763 and
the seizure of Orthodox Church properties: "For Catherine, these
events signaled a triumph of state over Church." In 1775, when
Smohozhevs'kyi was informed that in accordance with "Russian
custom" his Uniate Church communications would have to be officially countersigned, the archbishop bemoaned "such innovations
by means of which will be gradually eradicated all the customs
and rules of the ecclesiastical pastors."[24] This was clearly a conventional eighteenth-century lament against enlightened state
intervention, rather than any special cry of religious persecution.

Beyond these issues of Roman appeals and Russian counter-
signatures, Catherine's other major jurisdictional rearrangement
was her insistence on exactly one bishop for each of the Catholic
rites within her empire. Strict as she was about her political sovereignty, she wanted no scraps of her newly acquired territory,
freshly severed from the Commonwealth, to retain any religious
subordination to bishops in Poland. As Smohozhevs'kyi had been
told, she "would not suffer in her estates any bishop who was
not her subject." This model of one episcopal authority for each
religious community also corresponded to Catherine's enlightened notions of rational religious organization, for it seemed
to facilitate the exercise of her own sole secular authority over
subjects spiritually governed by one sole bishop. Maria Theresa
subscribed to a similarly unifying conception when in 1774 she
made of the Barbaraeum a seminary for the Uniate rites of Hun-
gary and Croatia, as well as Galicia. In the Russian Empire, the
annexed territory in Belarus roughly matched the old diocese of
Polatsk; thus, the concept of the single diocese would not become
a weapon of destruction until after the vast acquisitions of the
second and third partitions twenty years later. After 1772 there

---

24   Madariaga, *Russia in the Age of Catherine*, 512–14; John Alexander, *Catherine the Great: Life and Legend* (Oxford, 1989), 76–77; Smogorzewski, *Epistolae*, 173.

was, naturally, grumbling in Rome about the altered status quo, but, interestingly, the two bishops concerned—Smohozhevs´kyi for the Uniates and Siestrzeńcewicz for the Roman Catholics—seemed rather less distressed by a principle that actually enhanced their own authority. Smohozhevs´kyi, in fact, urged Rome to find a way to confirm canonically the new extent of his diocese, as Catherine had ordered, though he feared it might seem "almost as if I desired to dilate the borders of my pastorate," that he might appear to be "a usurper of the sheep of others."[25] Throughout this whole period of enlightened intervention in Russia, Austria, and Poland, there would always be certain elements of the Uniate Church that found particular innovations to their advantage—even at the cost of the status quo.

The Uniate Basilian monks registered other aspects of the shock of the partitions, in some cases even more forcefully than the bishops. "Today can count as the most terrible (*nayokropnieyszy*) in our lives," affirmed the Uniate Basilian monks of Polatsk in the monastery journal for 16 September 1772 (Julian calendar). For them the implications of the partition appeared, at least at first, to be something truly alarming, like a call to apocalyptic judgment:

> We monks, having said matins, were all peacefully in our cells attending to our monastic diversions, when around nine o'clock suddenly an alarm was trumpeted and the cloister bell ordered to be rung, to summon all the monks to gather in the church. Armed troops were parading in front of the church, and two trumpeters preceded them, continually sounding the trumpets... When we were gathered in the church in great fear and alarm, a colonel stood in the center of the church with other officers, and the troops were posted at the church doors.[26]

---

25   Smogorzewski, *Epistolae*, 91–92.

26   *Arkheograficheskii sbornik dokumentov otnosiashchikhsia k istorii Sievero-Zapadnoi Rusi*, vol. 10 (Vilnius, 1874), 365.

The frightened monks, feeling that their monastery had become the particular object of Russian military conquest, could not fail to feel with traumatic conviction that they were not in Poland anymore. They were presented with the orders of General Mikhail Krechetnikov for the lands newly annexed by Russia, requiring an oath of loyalty from all of Catherine's new subjects.

The Uniate Basilians were particularly distressed to learn they also were now expected to pray not only for Catherine and her heir, Grand Duke Paul, but also for the Orthodox Synod. Smohozhevs´kyi intervened by writing to Krechetnikov:

> Today, only because of the sinister fate of the world, I must remain alienated in this country from the sovereign government of the King of Poland, to whom I have always honestly maintained complete fidelity. So, in accordance with my obligation to my Church and to my sheep, I offer the oath of loyalty and obedience to the new government, and also prayers to God according to the formula given, as honesty and piety require it of me. But since I find in the same formula the duty to pray to God for the Synod, which is not of my confession, and can have no sovereignty over me, and detracts ipso facto from the obedience I owe to the Roman Pope, and thus deprives me of my Catholic faith, and with me so many priests and laymen, I cannot make a profession of that nature, and therefore I do not wish to present myself at the cathedral, and on the contrary I will gladly give myself up for arrest.[27]

Thus, he argued for the strict separation of his political and religious loyalties in the Russian Empire. Smohozhevs´kyi politely suggested to Krechetnikov that this formula was perhaps intended only for Orthodox Churches and mistakenly prescribed to the Uniates, but in fact this was surely one of those pitfalls to be found in "the perplexity of that one little word": Catholics. Catherine, in this case, seemed not to recognize the Uniates,

---

27   Smogorzewski, *Epistolae*, 61–62; *Arkheograficheskii sbornik*, 10:365–66.

with their Slavonic rite, as Catholics, and Smohozhevs´kyi had to underline the fact that the Synod was "not of my confession," that the formula "deprives me of my Catholic faith."

Krechetnikov went so far as to suggest that the most benign solution would be simultaneous prayers for the Synod and the pope, to which Smohozhevs´kyi replied that it would be "obvious foolishness" to recognize "two heads of one Church." After all, the one crucial consideration that made his "sheep" Catholics was the recognition of the absolute hierarchical authority of the pope as their supreme pastor. The Russian authorities gave way, and Smohozhevs´kyi communicated the amended policy to the Uniate clergy: "We pray, therefore, for Her Imperial Majesty and for her imperial heir, and we pray thus at the time and in the same manner as we used to pray for His Majesty the King of Poland," but "we must keep the visible Head of our faith, the Holy Pope of Rome, in our prayers without changing our custom...without the least mention of the Russian Synod."[28] Catherine's concession on this matter of prayers suggested that she was not, at this moment, fully committed to the harassment of her Uniate subjects.

Ironically, Smohozhevs´kyi's tenacious resistance to the proposed formula, with its implicit subordination to the Synod and alienation from Rome, must have owed something to the long experience of the Uniate bishops in Poland, where the Roman Catholic bishops had often plotted to gain hierarchical authority over their Uniate counterparts. Having gained his point, however, Smohozhevs´kyi organized a dinner for Krechetnikov and his officers on 20 September 1772 at the Basilian monastery, a first step toward reconciliation and reassurance after the alarming Russian military manifestation on 16 September. By 3 October the Polatsk monastery was hesitantly participating in the illuminations that marked the anniversary of Catherine's coronation ten years before, and by the end of November, with the arrival of Catherine's name day, the monks could casually report that "all

---

28   *Arkheograficheskii sbornik*, 10:367-69; Skinner, *Western Front*, 154-55.

Polatsk" was observing the occasion, including themselves. The Uniates were adapting themselves to the change of sovereignty perpetrated in the first partition.[29]

Though Smohozhevs´kyi had to accept certain changes that touched on his own episcopal authority and jurisdiction, the Uniate status quo in Belarus was left intact at the parish level. The archbishop was very much aware of his own focal role as the giver of oaths, leader of prayers, and Catherine's first Uniate subject. He wrote of "the vigilance at the place in which I live, the jealousy of the government that keeps its eye on me."[30] Catherine's eye was directly upon him when he made his journey to St. Petersburg in 1773 to render homage in person. There at court Catherine rose from cards to ask after his health, and inquire pointedly how he was doing with the Russian language. He must have been doing very well indeed, for his account of St. Petersburg was crammed full of social encounters, and he seems to have devoted himself wholeheartedly to making the connections that might be useful to his Church. He attended many dinners, and was impressed that in the November cold his hosts still managed to serve "the freshest grapes, the tastiest pears, artichokes, and watermelons." He also was impressed by Catherine's absolute power, and wrote to Rome afterwards to ask if the pope would consider sending her "some famous painting," and another for the Grand Duke Paul, the better to conciliate for Catholicism their invaluable favor.[31]

While Smohozhevs´kyi felt himself under the eye of an absolute government, he also had to provide an encyclopedic account of his Church for the purposes of enlightened administration. He was "tormented" in 1775 by the government's insistence on figures: the number of children of priests, the rates of parish taxation, all

---

29   *Arkheograficheskii sbornik*, 10:367–69.

30   Smogorzewski, *Epistolae*, 84; see also John LeDonne, *Ruling Russia: Politics and Administration in the Age of Absolutism, 1762-1796* (Princeton, 1984), 317–25.

31   Smogorzewski, *Epistolae*, 87, 95.

"grave and onerous matters." He felt the pressure of the spotlight again that same year when he celebrated in his cathedral a *Te Deum* for the anniversary of Catherine's victory over the Turks. Members of the provincial government were present for the occasion, but that was not enough for Smohozhevs´kyi: he had the sermon translated into Russian and rushed to St. Petersburg. "Everyone there may see that the Uniates know how to respect and honor the throne."[32] His performance of the part of the Uniate archiepiscopal subject was a tour de force, and Catherine remained well satisfied with him and his Church in the 1770s.

At the end of the decade, however, he was promoted to the metropolitanate in Poland, and the vacancy he left behind, after such an effective performance, turned into the first true crisis for the Uniates of Belarus in the Russian Empire. In 1780 Smohozhevs´kyi begged Chernyshev, with whom he had gotten along so well, to remind Catherine of his past service:

> With how much loyalty I always fulfilled the duties of a true Russian subject, with how much commitment I procured the education of the clergy, the institution of the seminary so desirable in that region, with how much expenditure I continued the enterprise of building, of gardens, of hemp, and of agriculture, all for the advantage of my archiepiscopal successors and as an ornament for the Russian land.[33]

He had learned perfectly the discourse appropriate to a subject of enlightened absolutism; here was an archbishop who measured his service to the state in terms of his educational and economic enterprises. In assuming the metropolitanate, however, he ceased to be Catherine's subject, and lost his claim upon her favor. The vacancy left by such a consummate ecclesiastical statesman

---

32   Smogorzewski, *Epistolae*, 173–75.

33   Smogorzewski, *Epistolae*, 227.

was one that Catherine would not be quick to fill, and therein lay the crisis.

Whatever Priest the Community Desires

In 1779 the Uniate metropolitan, Lev Sheptyts´kyi (Leon Szeptycki), died, and Smohozhevs´kyi was Stanisław August's candidate to succeed to the metropolitan diocese in Ukraine. This promotion to hierarchical supremacy within the Uniate Church was one that Smohozhevs´kyi relished all the more inasmuch as it would extract him from the Russian Empire and restore him to the Commonwealth. Carefully, he negotiated with St. Petersburg for a smooth succession to his own see at Polatsk, obtaining Catherine's preliminary approval for Bishop Ryllo of Chełm. Ryllo, however, had been harassed and arrested by Russian soldiers in Ukraine in 1774, and was not eager in 1779 to seize the opportunity to move to Polatsk. It turned out that he also had been soliciting from Maria Theresa an appointment to the see of Przemyśl in the Habsburg monarchy, which he now obtained and accepted instead of the Polatsk succession that had been arranged for him in the Russian Empire. "A bishop cannot follow his own comfort and pleasure," wrote the angry Warsaw nuncio, Giovanni Archetti, "without betraying his promises and obligations to God himself."[34] Ryllo, however, could and did. "I was powerfully surprised," commented Smohozhevs´kyi, "and immediately I began to foresee the worst possible effect for my own pastorate here, in view of such an evident contempt for the favors of this sovereign."[35] Catherine had been ready to accept Ryllo, and now her acceptance was spurned; he preferred the invitation of Maria Theresa.

Smohozhevs´kyi promptly presented for her consideration an alternative candidate to the fickle Ryllo: Porfyrii Vazhyns´kyi (Porfiriusz Ważyński), the protoarchimandrite of the Uniate Basil-

---

34   ANV 63, Archetti, 24 November 1779.

35   Smogorzewski, *Epistolae*, 227.

ian order. Catherine would not be won over so easily a second time. Smohozhevs´kyi then offered himself up to the tsarina, proposing to hold the metropolitanate and the see of Polatsk simultaneously, or at least to remain at Polatsk until a successor could be chosen. He emphasized this to Catherine through the language of courtship: without an appointed successor, how could he "abandon his first spiritual bride, and marry another."[36] He was hoping to make an impression on Catherine personally when she visited Polatsk in the spring of 1780, but, unluckily, he found himself feverishly ill on the one night he was supposed to dine in the imperial presence. He received instead a sickbed visit from the powerful Grigorii Potemkin, who drank chocolate while the ailing archbishop tried to speak persuasively about the succession in the diocese; Potemkin later sent a bottle of absinthe to fight the fever. The archbishop, sick in bed, was unembarrassed about appealing to the man in Catherine's bed, her current favorite, Aleksandr Lanskoi—though without results. "The fever has lifted, but weakness still keeps me in bed," noted Smohozhevs´kyi that summer, "but in the present circumstances it is not easy to cure a wounded heart."[37] His condition was medical, of course, but the circumstances were political, and the consequences spiritual; his health had kept him from meeting with Catherine at a critical moment for the Uniates.

It would not have made any difference. As far as she was concerned, Smohozhevs´kyi had ceased to be her subject from the moment he responded favorably to the offer of Stanisław August. "Now that he is a citizen and prelate of a foreign state," reasoned Catherine about Smohozhevs´kyi in 1780, "how can he serve two lords at the same time?" This had been one of her fundamental principles from the beginning in Belarus—"that she would not suffer in her estates any bishop who was not her subject"—and

36   Smogorzewski, *Epistolae*, 228.

37   *Akty izdavaemye Vilenskoiu arkheograficheskoiu kommissieiu*, vol. 16 (Vilnius, 1889), 395–97.

now she announced that he would have to refrain in the future from "mixing himself up in the spiritual affairs of our empire."[38] Setting spiritual affairs to one side, there then emerged a highly undignified controversy about some furniture that had been "transported clandestinely" out of the archiepiscopal residence in Polatsk and into Poland along with Smohozhevs′kyi. Was it his personal property, or did it belong to the diocese? He insisted that the removal had been done by "my subalterns, without my knowledge," but, concerned about his "reputation," he arranged for the disputed items to be returned to Russia.[39] Catherine insisted on a strict separation of the Uniate Church in Russia from the metropolitanate in Poland. She was determined that the archiepiscopal residence in Polatsk should retain all of its furnishings—though she still declined to allow for an archbishop to live in it.

The see remained vacant for four years, until 1783, and throughout that period there was great suspense—and no absence of provocative rumors—as to whom she would choose to fill the position. "Warsaw is full of reports that the Empress has nominated someone to the Polatsk archbishopric—but whom?" wrote Smohozhevs′kyi's correspondent in the Polish capital in 1780. "I would fervently like to find out!"[40] One dreaded possibility was that Catherine would try to install a Uniate who leaned toward Orthodoxy and would tilt the whole diocese in that direction. The Uniate Church was naturally on guard against such a possibility, since it was in similar fashion that some Orthodox dioceses—like Lviv and Przemyśl—had been brought over to the Union within the last century. Alternatively, it was feared that Catherine might subordinate her one Uniate diocese to her one Roman Catholic diocese, making the much-favored Siestrzeńcewicz the master of both. This, too, was a familiar menace for the Union, since Roman Catholic bishops had often sought the

---

38   Likowski, *Geschichte des allmaeligen Verfalls*, 1:196.

39   Smogorzewski, *Epistolae*, 262.

40   *Akty izdavaemye Vilenskoiu arkheograficheskoiu kommissieiu*, 16:325.

subordination of their Uniate episcopal colleagues in the Commonwealth. Ultimately, the worst possible outcome to be feared was that Catherine might actually appoint an Orthodox bishop to the Uniate see, and when Pope Pius VI wrote to her in 1780, begging her to fill the vacancy, he did not think it superfluous to specify that it be filled by a Uniate, not an Orthodox, bishop.[41]

After the partition of Poland, neither the Vatican nor the metropolitanate were eager to spell out the nominating powers of a non-Catholic sovereign ruling over a Catholic diocese. Catherine's prolonged refusal to fill the vacancy at Polatsk constituted a sort of investiture conflict inasmuch as she thus emphasized her own absolute authority in her own empire. When the pope wrote to her to plead that she fill the vacancy, the point was made that the see was hers to fill or not to fill. In fact, also in 1779, Maria Theresa, for all her Catholic piety, issued a decree to make a similar point about her rights of nomination in the Uniate dioceses acquired from Poland. In the controversy that raged within the Uniate Church over whether the new bishop of Lviv would be a Basilian monk or a secular priest, the Habsburg empress carefully emphasized her prerogative of choice and strictly disallowed any appeals for arbitration or dispensation from Rome.[42]

While Catherine refused to name an archbishop, the administration of the diocese in the interim was left in the hands of a three-man consistory of Uniate ecclesiastics. These gentlemen were in no position to exercise strong leadership: "We consult with each other about how we are to save so many souls. We find no means and even if there were such to be found, we would only bring down greater misfortune upon our necks."[43] They worried over whether to take refuge in the Roman Catholic Church and give up the Union as lost. In the meantime, in the absence of an

41   Johannes Madey, *Kirche zwischen Ost und West: Beiträge zur Geschichte der Ukrainischen und Weissruthenischen Kirche* (Munich, 1969), 102.

42   Madey, *Kirche zwischen Ost und West*, 117–18.

43   Likowski, *Geschichte des allmaeligen Verfalls*, 1:201.

archbishop, new Uniate priests were not being ordained, and Catherine issued an extraordinary ukaz to provide new parish priests when necessary:

> In case a Uniate community should be lacking its priest, or if one should die, the community should be questioned as to which faith they want for their priest, so that the government can install whatever priest the community desires.[44]

Such an experiment in liberty of conscience and such seeming deference to the community in choosing its own religion was rather rare in early modern Europe. It was both dramatically enlightened and, at the same time, by no means benevolent, for it was obviously designed to apply religious pressure on the Uniates—the paradoxical pressure of pretended religious democracy.

For Catherine it was a game: letting on that Belarus was the Rhode Island of Eastern Europe, an experiment in spiritual liberty, while knowing that her grand gesture could only harm the institutional Uniate Church—inasmuch as it could only lose communities, but not possibly gain new ones. In fact, since 1772, the Uniate Church in Belarus had been forbidden by decree to accept converts from Orthodoxy—consistent with the official Russian Orthodox position that such conversions had always been dishonestly contrived. In 1782 Catherine commented that, historically, the Uniates "adopted the Roman Communion only as the result of persecutions that they experienced in Poland and of the tricks of the Roman priests."[45]

Catherine, in thus toying with the peasants of Belarus and using them in her religious experiment, was demonstrating again that same somewhat nastily scientific curiosity about whether

---

44   Likowski, *Geschichte des allmaeligen Verfalls*, 1:205; from Augustin Theiner, *Neuesten Zustände der katholischen Kirche beider Ritus in Polen und Russland seit Katharina II* (Augsburg, 1840); Skinner, *Western Front*, 164.

45   Skinner, *Western Front*, 164–65.

they were really and truly "Catholic." If she applied the heat of religious freedom to the Uniate amalgam of ritual and dogma, would it separate out into its constituent elements (Roman Catholicism and Russian Orthodoxy), and what would be the proportions? While this experiment could only be viewed as a terrible menace by the Uniate Church, it also offered an extraordinary, historically precocious opportunity to have its peasant believers affirm their faith. Those communities that chose to remain in the Uniate Church passed through the trial of religious self-determination; they became bound and committed to their faith on a whole new, and distinctly modern, level. The circumstances of choice were, of course, susceptible to manipulation, and there were rumored to be Russian Orthodox agents who cleverly intoxicated their Uniate prey before proposing apostasy.[46] Smohozhevs´kyi, now in Poland, denounced Catherine's experiment as a "bloody" one, and believed that the Orthodox Synod was harassing his former flock by "fomenting trouble among the rough people, with good and with evil, with prayers, persuasions, and intoxication, with exemptions and with bastinadoes."[47] Thus, the Uniate Church faced institutional pressure from the continuing uncertainty about the vacant archbishopric, while the practice of Orthodox "persuasions" upon "the rough people" suggested the popular implications of Catherine's experiment with the Uniates.

According to one Uniate estimate in 1782, there were 100,000 souls lost (out of 800,000 Uniates in the Russian Empire); many were lost to Orthodoxy, and some opted for Roman Catholicism. The great majority of Uniates, however, held fast to the Union. Even with this unprecedented freedom of choice, which prevailed for the four years that the Polatsk see remained vacant, the great majority of the Uniates turned out to be "Catholics" after all. There were, to be sure, the most dire predictions from the presiding consistory: "If a supreme pastor is not chosen soon, there will

---

46   Likowski, *Geschichte des allmaeligen Verfalls*, 1:200.

47   Smogorzewski, *Epistolae*, 260.

remain no one over whom he can exercise his pastoral office."[48] This gloomy forecast in 1780 was based on the uncertainty of the future; what no one could know, at that time, was that the crisis was only an interval. In 1783 a new archbishop would take office, and the Uniate Church in the Russian Empire would achieve a new stability for the decade to come.

In the agony of uncertainty the consistory sent its appeals across the border to Poland, and from there new appeals were formulated by Smohozhevs´kyi at the metropolitanate and Archetti at the nunciature. Though they did not think of the Ottoman sultan this time around, they hoped to influence Catherine by bringing into play the goodwill of Stanisław August and Maria Theresa. The Habsburg empress, to their great regret, died right in the middle of the crisis in 1780, but Smohozhevs´kyi, recognizing her as "the most special protectress" of the Uniates, still hoped that "with her supremely great merits even in heaven she may defend my poor Uniates." As for Joseph, now the sole ruler in Vienna, he could easily intercede "with only two little words": status quo.[49] Aside from the almost comical misapprehension of Joseph as a champion of the status quo, the strategy was more fundamentally misguided, since what lay behind the crisis all along was Catherine's interest in her own imperial authority over Church affairs, and appeals to foreign sovereigns could only aggravate her sensitivity in this regard. The true issues and dimensions of the crisis finally emerged in the course of the remarkable correspondence that ensued between the tsarina and the pope.

When Pope Pius VI personally wrote to Catherine in 1780 to protest the vacancy at Polatsk, a grand gesture from the very summit of the Catholic Church, her reply of 1781 brushed aside his concern for the Uniates and asked the pope to create a Roman Catholic archbishopric at Mahiliou̇ (Mogilev) for Siestrzeńcewicz. This peremptory demand from a non-Catholic sovereign for an

---

48   Likowski, *Geschichte des allmaeligen Verfalls*, 1:202–3.

49   Smogorzewski, *Epistolae*, 268.

archbishopric cut to suit her fancy demonstrated that she was determined to establish her own authority over the Catholic Church in her empire. Since she made her demand for a Roman Catholic archbishop in response to the pope's demand for a Uniate archbishop, the issues became linked, as she intended; it was to be a matter of quid pro quo, not status quo. Siestrzeńcewicz, however, was no favorite in Rome, especially because he had, as Catherine wished, encouraged the survival of the Jesuits in the Russian Empire in defiance of the papal suppression of 1773. In a letter of 1781 Pius refused to create the archbishopric Catherine wanted for Siestrzeńcewicz, and she replied in 1782 that she had created it herself by decree; the pope only needed to send the archiepiscopal pallium for a properly ceremonial investiture. Now she had even more flagrantly trespassed on papal authority. Her letter mentioned, by the way, that the Uniates were "just a little flock," perhaps too few to require an archbishop of their own. The quid pro quo had become a matter of threat, and, as in Ukraine ten years before, the Uniate Church served as a pressure point for Catherine in obtaining other satisfactions. "Powerful sovereign," she wrote, mockingly, for the pope was not powerful at all, "we do not doubt that our care for the good of the Roman Church in our empire will be agreeable to you."[50]

The pope, who had seemed to stress the importance of the Uniates by taking up his pen on their behalf, now found their crisis to be less of a priority when it had to be weighed against other concessions. Furthermore, at this critical moment in the correspondence, Pius suddenly had no attention to spare for Russian affairs, inasmuch as he was fully occupied with the Josephine reforms in the Habsburg Empire and his own papal journey to Vienna to protest. When Catherine had received no reply from Rome by the end of 1782, her sense of self-importance was wound-

50   Larry Wolff, *The Vatican and Poland in the Age of the Partitions: Diplomatic and Cultural Encounters at the Warsaw Nunciature* (Boulder and New York, 1988), 173; ANV 65, Catherine II to Pius VI, 30 January 1782.

ed again, and it was then that she menacingly gave out the word that Catholicism in Russia could be eliminated altogether; the Uniates needed "only the least signal to embrace our Orthodox religion." In 1783 the pope agreed to all her demands, sending Archetti as legate from Warsaw to St. Petersburg to present her with the pallium for Siestrzeńcewicz, as specified.

Archetti, at the Warsaw nunciature, was far more frightened by the Uniate crisis than anyone in Rome. "Every travail and every pain that I have experienced in recent years, when something sinister happened to the Church," he wrote in 1780, "seems like nothing in comparison to the affliction which oppresses me now."[51] While on the one hand he underestimated the steadfastness of the Uniates, on the other hand he appreciated the innovativeness of Catherine's assault in the context of the "sinister" age of the Enlightenment. From Warsaw, Archetti attempted to mediate the correspondence between Pius and Catherine in such a way as to avoid confrontation, for he feared that the fate of the Uniates in Russia could jeopardize their position in Poland as well: "The tsarina dominates here almost as in Russia." As soon as Catherine put forward demands of her own, Archetti counseled concession, urging Rome to save the Uniates by accepting Siestrzeńcewicz "as if the Jesuit matter were not at all mixed up in this."[52] Above all, from Warsaw, he was in a perfect position to appreciate Catherine's irresistible power: "If she doesn't get her way, we will go on losing the souls of that most numerous population (which is not 'a little flock'), and soon enough they will all run to their eternal ruin."[53] Thus, when Archetti was chosen as legate to St. Petersburg, he was determined to reverse Rome's futile resistance and to gratify Catherine at all costs in order to obtain the desired Uniate appointment at Polatsk. Rome had grave doubts about

---

51   Wolff, *Vatican and Poland*, 164–65; ANV 63, 29 March 1780.

52   Wolff, *Vatican and Poland*, 169, 174; ANV 64, Archetti, 28 March 1781; ANV 65, Archetti, 2 October 1782.

53   ANV 65, Archetti, 6 March 1782.

whether it was appropriate for a papal legate to kiss the hand of the tsarina; Archetti had none. He stayed in St. Petersburg for almost a year without saying a word to Catherine about the controversial continuation of the Jesuits, and when he left in 1784 he had secured his cardinalate, as well as Catherine's good opinion ("a thoroughly good child"—she thought he should be pope), not to mention a splendid sable fur coat.[54] He also left behind him in Russia a new Uniate archbishop at Polatsk.

Catherine had agreed at last, and Archetti, while he was still in St. Petersburg in 1783, hastened to arrange for Iraklii Lisovsʹkyi (Herakliusz Lisowski), a member of the Polatsk consistory, to be installed as the new archbishop. The crisis was over. Of all its remarkable aspects, not least was the ease of its ending. The affair began with Ryllo's affront to Catherine's vanity; it ended with Archetti graciously kissing her hand. More important, it began when Catherine wanted to make a point about her absolute authority over Church affairs in her empire, and ended when that had been explicitly recognized. She herself capped the crisis with an ukaz of 1783 that formally removed the archbishop of Polatsk from any shadow of hierarchical subordination to the metropolitan in Poland. Still, what remained the most important message of the whole affair was that Catherine could apply pressure to the Uniates in pursuit of other interests, and release the pressure when she was ready. It had happened in Ukraine at the time of the first partition, and now in Belarus again. The pattern was a menacing one, but the outcome in both cases suggested that Catherine was not fully committed to the elimination of the Uniates. Their religious faith excited her malicious curiosity, while their Church remained a pawn in her game of strategic secular statecraft, according to the conventions of enlightened absolutism.

---

54   Paul Pierling, *La Russie et le Saint-Siège*, vol. 5 (Paris, 1912), 155–57.

Josephus II

In 1780 the Uniate Church lamented the passing of Maria Theresa, "most special protectress," and could only hope that Joseph would not hesitate to invoke those "two little words"—status quo—on behalf of the Polatsk diocese in Russia. In 1782 the pope postponed the urgent business of responding to Catherine about Russian affairs, because he was otherwise preoccupied with Joseph's unprecedented assault on Church prerogatives in the Habsburg lands. Between 1780, when Joseph took over as sole ruler, and 1782, when he received Pius in Vienna to hear the papal expostulations, an unprecedented religious revolution took place in the Habsburg lands. The approximately 1.5 million Uniates assigned to the Habsburgs in 1772 found their status quo more significantly transformed than did the half as many Uniates of the Russian Empire who were, during precisely these years of the early 1780s, feeling the pressure of the vacancy at Polatsk. In fact, Catherine pursued her religious policy in consultation with a professor of canon law from Vienna, who came to Moscow to teach and brought with him the principles of Josephinism.[55] Just as Catherine's fundamental concerns were connected to state authority over Church affairs, the Josephine reforms were even more nakedly devoted to precisely that agenda.

Maria Theresa, though certainly a devout Catholic, was herself interested in defining imperial authority with respect to Rome, and in the last year of her reign she did keep the Vatican out of the process of the Uniate succession to the see of Lviv. She would allow no appeal for Roman dispensations in the controversy over who was eligible for the Uniate episcopacy, nor in the equally heated controversy over Uniate transit to Roman Catholicism. It has been argued that in Galicia in particular—a brand new Habsburg acquisition—she cooperated with Joseph in the 1770s

---

55   Albert M. Ammann, *Abriss der ostslawischen Kirchengeschichte* (Vienna, 1950), 443.

to pave the way for the big religious reforms of the 1780s.[56] Certainly the Uniates themselves appreciated the importance of her central authority in Vienna, and the bishop of Lviv went so far as to keep a representative in the capital to lobby at court in the controversy over creating an ecclesiastical chapter for the Lviv cathedral. As for the bishop himself, Lev Sheptyts´kyi, the empress permitted him to assume the metropolitanate in Poland in 1778 while retaining the Lviv see in Austria; thus she conceded the international unity of the Uniate Church which Catherine would not countenance when Smohozhevs´kyi sought an analogous position after Sheptyts´kyi's death in 1779.

Maria Theresa, however, published a formal imperial rescript in 1778 in order to make perfectly clear that Sheptyts´kyi's joint tenure was a question of her favor:

> Since we have learned that your devotion has brought you to the dignity of the metropolitanate, so do we hereby testify to our most gracious satisfaction at this advancement of your devotion, and furthermore confirm with all the more pleasure our most gracious protection. We may have well-founded confidence, based on your devout zeal to carry out our commands, that by these qualities you will bring about all the more quickly and completely whatever appears necessary to us for the improvement of Church discipline and the worldly well-being of our Greek Catholic subjects.[57]

Here Maria Theresa made Sheptyts´kyi's ecclesiastical career very much the business of the Habsburg state, praising in particular his

---

56   Anton Korczok, *Die griechisch-katholische Kirche in Galizien* (Leipzig and Berlin, 1921), 54; from Władysław Chotkowski, *Historya Polityczna Kościoła w Galicyi* (Cracow, 1909); see also Larry Wolff, *Idea of Galicia*, 13–62; and Larry Wolff, "Inventing Galicia: Messianic Josephinism and the Recasting of Partitioned Poland," *Slavic Review*, Vol. 63, No. 4 (Winter 2004), 818–40.

57   Pelesz, *Geschichte der Union*, 2:569; from Michael Harasiewicz, *Annales Ecclesiae Ruthenae* (Lviv, 1862).

"zeal" in obeying her commands, and presenting his new Polish responsibilities as a mere Austrian convenience—inasmuch as he could use the power of the metropolitanate to advance her subjects in Galicia. The balance between bishop and empress was becoming a delicate one, and was never really tested since Sheptyts´kyi died the next year, and Maria Theresa passed away the year after that. Certainly the empress was not inhibited about making demands on her Uniate bishops. Even in her celebrated act of beneficence, the creation of the Barbaraeum, the Uniate bishops were taxed for the support of their seminarians in Vienna—and they strenuously protested the imposition.[58]

Joseph would give all his bishops much more reason to protest. Unlike Maria Theresa, he was no pious Catholic. Though he was ten years younger than Catherine, they were of the same generation of enlightened absolutism: Joseph joined his mother as co-ruler in 1765, three years after Catherine herself ascended the Russian throne in a coup d'état, possibly complicit in the murder of her husband the tsar. Joseph appreciated Catherine's adherence to the Petrine tradition of state over Church, but his own reforms were so radical that they gave her new ideas. Perhaps the most fundamental difference between Catherine and Joseph with regard to the Uniate Church was that the Habsburg religious reforms were directed against all Catholic institutions. Catholicism in Austria was the dominant religion, and the Uniates of Galicia were blown about almost incidentally in a storm that overturned the much grander edifice of Roman Catholicism. Catherine, on the other hand, when she came to the throne in 1762, found the dominant religion, Orthodoxy, already reasonably well regulated by the state. The Uniate diocese she acquired from Poland in 1772 was institutionally independent by comparison, and so her interventions acted upon the Uniates particularly, inevitably becoming acts of discrimination. Joseph's interventions had the opposite effect: by assaulting the Uniate Church in conjunction

---

58   Madey, *Kirche zwischen Ost und West*, 120.

with his assault on Catholicism in general, he forced upon the Uniates an irresistible inclusion.

Thus, while it is possible to enumerate individually Catherine's decrees for the Uniates of Belarus, the Uniates of Galicia were affected by all those general reforms that constituted the Josephine revolution. The famous Toleration Patent of 1781 gave protection to the Uniates' traditional rivals, the Orthodox, a minority in Galicia. The secularization of the monasteries and dissolution of the orders, beginning in 1781, spared only those that provided education and cared for the sick, and took a toll on the Uniate Basilians. From 1782 Joseph redefined and reorganized the dioceses and all their constituent parishes, ultimately aiming to make Austrian ecclesiastics into salaried civil servants. State seminaries were created to educate the clergy under government supervision. Strict regulation by decree affected every aspect of religious life from the very highest matters of papal pronouncements and relations with Rome, to the smallest details of ritual, devotion, and decoration in each parish church.

For the Uniates of Galicia the crucial Josephine institution was the General Seminary in Lviv. It was one of a set of seminaries the emperor established throughout the Habsburg lands in his determination to control the education of the clergy. They were, for the most part, unpopular and unsuccessful, and after Joseph's death they were generally closed down by his brother and successor, Leopold II. The one exception was Lviv, where the seminary met a pressing need for more and better clerical training. The price for the General Seminary was the Barbaraeum; Maria Theresa's Viennese establishment was closed in 1784, right after Joseph opened his own in Lviv in 1783 by court decree. The other casualty was the Theatine College in Lviv, exactly the sort of seminary Joseph was most eager to displace. In 1787 he further expanded educational opportunities by creating the Ruthenian Institute, which offered clerical instruction in the vernacular language for those who could not study in Latin at the General Seminary.

In 1790, when Leopold was already abolishing the Josephine seminaries in Austria, the Uniate bishops of Galicia petitioned for the preservation of the Lviv institution as an exception—and the emperor, by decree, allowed it to continue. It was not that the bishops failed to appreciate the significance of state control, for they also eagerly petitioned to take over from the government the administration and supervision of the seminary. Leopold, however, would not go that far, and, in fact, the bishops thought it worth preserving the Josephine institution even at the cost of continuing state supervision. For just as Catherine's scruples about foreign bishops in her empire served to extend the authority of her own Uniate bishop at Polatsk, so Joseph's insistence on brand new Habsburg seminaries also allowed his Uniate bishops in Galicia to make themselves more powerful within their Uniate Church. Petro Bilians´kyi (Piotr Bielański), bishop of Lviv, had succeeded Sheptyts´kyi in 1780, chosen by Maria Theresa without reference to the Vatican; at the same time Ryllo came to Przemyśl, insulting Catherine by refusing Polatsk, and thereby causing great distress in Rome. These were new bishops for the Josephine decade, and Joseph, by removing Uniate education from the Viennese Barbar-aeum and Lviv Theatine College, enabled these rising episcopal powers in Galicia to join with him in shaping the next generation of Uniate clergy. After twenty-five years the General Seminary was finally turned over to complete episcopal control; in 1806 Emperor Francis I put it in the hands of Antin Anhelovych (Anton Anhelowicz), the head of the newly created metropolitanate of Halych. There was, however, one crucial connection that made this a difficult shift to interpret: Anhelovych, some twenty-five years before, had been Joseph's first state-appointed rector for the new General Seminary. Thus, it is not easy to say whether the Uniate Church took over the Josephine Seminary, or whether the Josephine Seminary took over the Uniate Church.

State intervention thus proved favorable or unfavorable for different elements within the Church. The General Seminary and Ruthenian Institute favored the Josephine bishops and created a new generation of priests, while the Basilian order lost its educational edge. Candidates for the order were put through the Seminary along with everyone else, while the Basilians' own schools tottered in the storm of Joseph's aggressive educational interests. The emperor's sweeping assault on the monasteries was even more damaging, and the establishment of imperial authority confirmed the subordination of the Basilians. In 1780, the first year of his sole reign, the order recognized the significance of Habsburg sovereignty by making the monks of Galicia into one distinct provincial division. In 1782 Joseph forced them one step further by disallowing the dependence of any monastery in Galicia upon the protoarchimandrite in Poland. Joseph did not formally sever the Uniates in general from the Commonwealth metropolitanate, as Catherine did in 1783, but his handling of the Basilians illustrated the same principle. The monks, now cut loose from their general, were placed under the authority of the Josephine bishops in Galicia, whose power correspondingly increased. Furthermore, though these bishops remained, for the time being, subject to the metropolitan in Poland, the idea for an independent Habsburg metropolitan, finally achieved in 1806, had already been seriously proposed and considered in 1779 at the death of Sheptys´kyi, and then again in 1790 at the death of Joseph.

In general, the emperor's assumption of power over the Church also enhanced the power of the bishops, since, like Catherine, Joseph built up their authority even while establishing his own over them. He bestowed upon Bilians´kyi and Ryllo supervisory consistories of lay officials, and the priests of both cathedrals, along with the consistory officials, were to bear the distinctive honorary insignia of a pectoral cross, Greek-style with equal arms. The men of Lviv had images of the Virgin and St. George on their crosses, while the men of Przemyśl had John the Baptist on theirs. In both cathedrals the crosses bore the inscription "Josephus II"—for these were not only the bishop's men, but also the emperor's.[59]

Patriotic Loyalty and Religious Zeal

While Joseph in the 1780s was already attempting to legislate a revolutionary state-controlled Church—a decade ahead of the French Civil Constitution of the Clergy—in Poland the Uniate Church still approached the monarch in the spirit of the ancien régime. In 1781 there took place in Warsaw a ceremonial laying of the first stone for a new Uniate church. Under that stone, the nuncio laid five Roman medallions honoring the pope, while Stanisław August, present for the occasion, added a silver medallion with his own effigy.[60] This emblematic conjunction of pope and king (in the imbalanced ratio of five to one) was a far cry from labeling the churchmen of Galicia with the tag "Josephus II." In Poland, the Uniate Church was still seeking the patronage of the state, whereas in Austria the state had gone far beyond patronage in its overwhelming impositions.

In 1783, just two years after the first stone in Warsaw, Smohozhevs´kyi was already expecting great things from the new church, which he placed in the context of the Uniates' tribulations in Ukraine ten years before:

> I have directed all my cares to that vast province of Ukraine, which
> forms the greater portion of the metropolitanate. In that time
> I have established myself in those parts, where until now no other
> metropolitan has ever made his residence, and I am procuring with
> my presence and my live voice to retain in the Holy Union those
> many populations that, after being seduced by the violence and
> fraud of the schismatics in the recent most unhappy turbulence
> of Ukraine, have now spontaneously returned in great number to

---

59   Madey, *Kirche zwischen Ost und West*, 118.

60   Wolff, *Vatican and Poland*, 170; ANV 64, Archetti, 16 May 1781.

the Catholic faith, and I go on recalling to the breast of the Church those most obstinate apostates who still persist in schism. The Lord blessing my pastoral cares, the Holy Union increases its numbers more and more in Ukraine, while I seek also to increase its splendor in every place, and particularly in the capital of the kingdom where many Uniates permanently reside. Therefore, for their ease, and for the decorum of our rite I have had constructed in Warsaw a spacious and elegant church, where in the future all the holidays shall be celebrated with the greatest solemnity.[61]

Here Smohozhevs'kyi gave a very clear idea of his program for the Uniates in post-partition Poland. He had assumed the metropolitanate just three years before in 1780, but his predecessors had never been able to think programmatically. Felitsian Pylyp Volodkovych (Felicjan Filip Wołodkowicz), who lived until 1778, had had his competence questioned too often and too controversially to be able to lead his Church into a new era after 1772. His successor Sheptyts'kyi survived only a year in the office, and even in that time retained his ties to Lviv and Maria Theresa. When Catherine refused to allow Smohozhevs'kyi to keep one foot in Polatsk, she gave wholly to the Commonwealth an extremely effective ecclesiastical statesman, one who had just graduated from an arduous political training in her own empire. At last in 1780 the Uniates of Ukraine would see their "spontaneous" recovery, which began in 1775, consolidated by thoroughgoing episcopal leadership.

The hallmark of Smohozhevs'kyi's statesmanship was his recognition that the flock required not only his pastoral leadership in Ukraine but, at the same time, his political influence in Warsaw. The man who had traveled to St. Petersburg to wait on Catherine at her card table knew well the importance of a royal capital in an age of enlightened absolutism. He had enjoyed the patronage of Stanisław August before 1772, before his diocese was partitioned away from the Commonwealth, and so in 1780

---

61   Smogorzewski, *Epistolae*, 307.

he returned to the royal favor of a monarch less treacherous to deal with than Catherine had been. In 1781 Stanisław August was there for the laying of the first stone of the Warsaw edifice; its "elegance" and "decorum" would impress upon the royal government the importance of the Uniate Church. Until his death in 1788, Smohozhevs´kyi pursued this dual policy of pastoral presence in Ukraine and political presence in Warsaw.

The year of his death was also, coincidentally, the year that his careful courting of the monarchy became almost irrelevant, as 1788 was the first year of the Four-Year Sejm, introducing a period of revolutionary upheaval in the Church affairs of the Commonwealth. At the Sejm, the Polish domain of the Uniate Church would finally feel the force of that state intervention which the Uniates of Belarus had first felt in the 1770s and the Uniates of Galicia still more deeply in the 1780s. The most celebrated act of the Sejm with regard to the Uniate Church redeemed a promise made two centuries before at the time of the Union: the metropolitan was admitted into the Senate of the Commonwealth, and thus permitted to join the Roman Catholic bishops. The Uniate parish clergy also had reason to praise the beneficence of the Sejm when it repealed the statute of 1764 that made the sons of Uniate priests liable to serfdom.

These gestures were intended to strike down the discriminatory barrier that had made the Uniate Church into a secondary stepsister of Roman Catholicism through two centuries of Polish history. Every bit as important, however, were those legislative measures that affected both forms of Catholicism and reordered their relations to the state. The crux of the matter was the clergy's inability to shelter its property from the revenue needs of the newly assertive state, especially as the Sejm sought to raise a great army for the future defense of Polish independence. In the spring of 1789 the ecclesiastical estate gave in to pressures for a doubled tax contribution, but far more important in principle was the act of July 1789 whereby the Sejm approved a formula for confiscating the property of the bishops and compensating them with state pensions. Under the unassuming title "Funds for the Army," debated and voted even as the French revolutionaries were storming the Bastille, each diocese was scheduled for economic liquidation at the death of its present bishop, though that was modified in 1790 to allow for the retention of some episcopal property.[62] This legislative claim upon the dioceses naturally encouraged further interventions in their affairs, including a program of administrative rationalization and the envisioning of state seminaries on the Josephine model. The interest of the Sejm in a new Uniate diocese at Minsk came from the need to provide for those parts of the Polatsk diocese remaining in Poland since 1772. Catherine in 1783 formally forbade her archbishop of Polatsk any connection to the metropolitanate in Poland, and now the Sejm, reciprocally, sought to sever all relations between Uniate parishes in Poland and the see of Polatsk in Russia.

These measures of the Sejm were intended to bind the Uniates to the Commonwealth under the new constitution of 1791. Such concerns naturally emerged at a moment when Poland was declaring its independence from Russia, and Catherine, after she invaded Poland in 1792, overturned every act of the Sejm. While enlightened absolutism in Russia and Austria, as far as the Uniates were concerned, would be judged according to the historical consequences for future generations, in Poland it could only be judged on its own terms—for the Commonwealth really did not have a future. The stillborn reforms of the Sejm fully reflected the values and concerns that the Enlightenment brought to matters of Church and state. Furthermore, not since Garampi's unheeded *Exposé* at the Partition Sejm twenty years before was there such a concerned discussion of Uniate religious affiliation and political loyalty as there was at the Four-Year Sejm.

---

62   Richard Butterwick, *The Polish Revolution and the Catholic Church, 1788-1792: A Political History* (Oxford: Oxford University Press, 2012), 79–101; Wolff, *Vatican and Poland*, 188–96.

While the constitution of 3 May 1791 left Catholicism, Roman and Uniate, as the dominant religion of the new regime, and the admission of the metropolitan to the Senate lent credibility to that dual dominance, at the same time the Sejm legislated the establishment of a state-sponsored Orthodox Church in the Commonwealth. Just as Catherine had insisted on a Uniate see at Polatsk fully independent of the metropolitanate in Poland, so the Sejm now reciprocally mandated an autocephalous Orthodox hierarchy in Poland with no ties to Moscow, directly subordinate to the Greek patriarch in Constantinople—approved by the Sejm in spite of Uniate anxieties and remonstrations.[63] The autocephalous Orthodox hierarchy was, however, no mere abstract exercise in assertive Commonwealth sovereignty, but rather a carefully considered response by the Sejm to eruptions of violence and counterrevolutionary conspiracies in Ukraine in 1789. This dangerous instability of the southeastern lands of the Commonwealth forced the Sejm to pay special attention to the Uniate and Orthodox populations of those lands, and to consider their institutional and sentimental relations to the Commonwealth state.

The religious unrest in Ukraine in 1768, promoted by Haidamak violence, had facilitated Russian intervention in the Commonwealth. Now in 1789, with the Sejm in session, the Commonwealth was gripped by what historian Barbara Skinner has characterized as a "Great Fear" (comparable to that of the French Revolution), with Polish suspicion of foreign knife peddlers from Russia creating apprehensions that there might be an uprising and massacre on Orthodox Easter. The Sejm immediately instituted an investigative commission to get to the bottom of the matter, and, to no one's surprise, uncovered the activity of Russian agents, with stocks of weapons hidden away in an Orthodox monastery. The Orthodox bishop, Viktor Sadkovs´kyi, was arrested. The Sejm's

---

63   Skinner, *Western Front*, 191–93; Butterwick, *Polish Revolution and the Catholic Church*, 300–311.

commission, however, also heard reports that Uniate priests were involved in the same conspiracies against Poland. Indeed, Uniate priests denounced other Uniate priests for collusion with Russian agents; the whole consistory of the diocese of Lutsk fell under suspicion, many others were arrested, and a few were even sentenced to death in the hasty justice that sought to squash incipient disorder. To be sure, the final report of 1790 blamed the Orthodox Church. Furthermore, the Lutsk ecclesiastic, Teodosii Brodovych (Teodozy Brodowicz), wrote a scathing indictment of the commission's readiness to believe the worst about the Uniates on the weakest evidence; he contemptuously cited the ignorance of the commissioners who mistook the Slavonic prayers to the "Tsarytsia," the Virgin Queen, for devotion to the "Tsarina" in St. Petersburg.[64] Brodovych, being from Lutsk, was himself suspect, and his self-justification pointed to the problematic persistence of some Polish suspicion of the Uniates, on the one hand, and some Uniate ambivalence about their own religious and political affiliations, on the other.

The Four-Year Sejm was concerned with the easing of religious tensions in the hope of reconciling the peoples of the Commonwealth in a common Polish patriotism. A declaration of the Sejm concerning religion in 1790 denounced "fanaticism" and urged the cause of "enlightenment" (oświecenie). The Sejm called upon "bishops of both rites to order the clergy, in a manner appropriate to every intelligence, most often and most particularly to illuminate (oświecać) the people concerning these important truths, which are very well known to elevated knowledge, that, on the strength of God's religion, loyalty to their own country is the most holy obligation." Thus Roman Catholic and Uniate bishops were particularly singled out and charged with bringing this patriotic message to their flocks. The Sejm offered an even broader vision of religious reconciliation, based on a policy of official toleration,

---

64   Likowski, *Geschichte des allmaeligen Verfalls*, 1:256–57; Skinner, *Western Front*, 183–91.

such that all those differentiated by religion "should be joined in love of country, loving one another, and living together in unity."[65] Freedom for Protestant and Orthodox worship would be protected, but Roman Catholic and Uniate populations were clearly regarded as the dual and principal targets for establishing patriotism through religious mobilization and illumination.

A special deputation of the Sejm reported on the state of the Union in Poland, beginning with the most elementary observations: "The Union in Poland forms part of the dominant religion. Neither in their dogma nor in their supreme head do the Greek Catholics differ from the Latin Catholics." This had to be set clearly before the Sejm, even two hundred years after the Union of Brest, as if these points might have failed to register on the government of the Commonwealth. "Through the negligence of the government the higher Uniate clergy was excluded from participation in the government and the lower clergy from its protection." This could now be rectified—by bringing the metropolitan into the Senate and protecting the children of parish priests from serfdom—and such attentions were justified by certain complex political considerations. "The neglect of the Uniates," the deputation remarked, "can only bind them to the Orthodox in insidious deceptions, and cause harm to the fatherland."[66] This was very close to the political appreciation of the Union that Garampi had attempted to publicize twenty years before. Now, a revolutionary constitutional regime, founded on the premise of national reform in defiance of foreign domination, necessarily weighed with new seriousness the affections and disaffections of its population. A broader conception of citizenship went hand in hand with a more intense interest in patriotic identity, marking

---

65   *Arkheograficheskii sbornik dokumentov otnosiashchikhsia k istorii Sievero-Zapadnoi Rusi*, vol. 5 (Vilnius, 1871), 246; Butterwick, *Polish Revolution and the Catholic Church*, 212–15; see also Butterwick, "Deconfessionalization," 91–121.

66   Likowski, *Geschichte des allmaeligen Verfalls*, 1:263.

a milestone in the emergence of of modern national affiliation. Traditional suspicions of the Uniates lent urgency to the question of how they would "bind" themselves, religiously and nationally.

The recently deceased Smohozhevs´kyi was hailed in the report of the deputation as a Polish national hero, demonstrating the perfect combination of "patriotic loyalty and religious zeal."[67] He had stood up to Catherine during the years when the Commonwealth was prostrate, when the government of Poland had no attention to spare for the Uniates. No mention was made of the fact that he had conciliated Catherine as much as he stood up to her, though the deputation concluded that Smohozhevs´kyi "might have been able to achieve greater success if he could have participated in the Senate of the Commonwealth." Therefore, "what he could not be, his successor will become." The deputation actually recommended the admission of all the Uniate bishops to the Senate, but the Sejm voted for the metropolitan alone, Teodosii Rostots´kyi (Teodozy Rostocki), and assigned him, in spite of his archiepiscopal status, a place of lesser precedence behind the Roman Catholic bishops. Historian Richard Butterwick has observed that, in the Sejm's Uniate concerns, "the political imperative had to battle with social prejudice." The metropolitan's admission was explained in the Sejm as a vindication of past promises, and also a "proof of favor to the clergy of that rite, who have distinguished themselves by unshakable loyalty to the king and the fatherland."[68] Actually, the encouragement and confirmation of that loyalty was the reason for Rostots´kyi's inclusion, but the continued exclusion of all the other Uniate bishops made the proof of favor less completely persuasive. By admitting the metropolitan alone, the Sejm showed itself, in fact, fully attuned to contemporary enlightened policy toward the Uniate Church. Catherine, too, had insisted on one archbishop alone

---

67 Likowski, *Geschichte des allmaeligen Verfalls*, 1:264.

68 Likowski, *Geschichte des allmaeligen Verfalls*, 1:264; Butterwick, *Polish Revolution and the Catholic Church*, 191 and 322.

to govern her Uniate subjects, while in Austria the possibility of a metropolitan for Galicia was already under consideration. The Uniates' ambiguous position between the worlds of Catholicism and Orthodoxy made it seem all the more urgent that there be one hierarchical head to speak for them clearly before the secular state—and relay its requirements clearly back to them.

In establishing political prerogatives over religious institutions, governments valued ecclesiastical structures that encouraged rational integration and organization. An emphasis on hierarchical authority was one aspect of this, while the rationalization of the dioceses and parishes was another, in Poland after 1788 as in Austria after 1780. The proposed establishment of a new see at Minsk was fully in accord with these principles. The deputation of the Sejm reported:

> The bishops assigned to foreign lands should have no jurisdiction in our land, and likewise our bishops should have none in neighboring states. They should be able to operate as officials, together with the civil government, and thus become witnesses to the intentions of the government.[69]

The first point of jurisdiction was almost a conventional one by that time, but the second point that followed from it, envisioning bishops who "operate as officials," represented the more radical implications of Josephinism and the French Constitution of the Clergy. This was very much a part of the religious policy of the Sejm, with its interest in appropriating diocesan property and paying salaries to the propertyless bishops. Such invasive policies were considered for Catholicism in general, but they were especially interesting in the case of the Uniate Church, since new paths of political reflection revealed the urgency of binding the Uniates to the doomed Commonwealth.

---

69   Likowski, *Geschichte des allmaeligen Verfalls*, 1:263-64.

A Few Signatures from the Community

The issue of Poland's political sovereignty stimulated the Four-Year Sejm to reconsider relations between the state and the Uniate Church, and, after Catherine's cancellation of the Sejm and violation of Polish sovereignty, she, too, attempted to transform state relations with the Uniates in the Russian Empire. Interventionist sponsorship of the Uniates in Poland never had time to take effect, since the Commonwealth expired in 1795, while interventionist harassment in the Russian Empire also failed to have its full effect, since Catherine died in 1796.

In fact, the whole interval from 1788, the first year of the Sejm, until Catherine's death in 1796 was one of rollercoaster turns in Russian-Polish relations. Just as in the previous period of unsettlement and reorientation from 1768 to 1775, now again the Uniate Church was buffeted about in conditions of political instability, and served as a convenient pressure point for Catherine as she found herself once again reconsidering her Polish policy. The Uniates in 1772 found themselves divided among three states, no longer united under the protection of the Commonwealth; after 1795 the Commonwealth ceased to exist altogether and the Uniates were vulnerable survivors of the state that had helped create their Church exactly two centuries earlier. At the same time, a radicalization of ideas about religious policy throughout Europe, already evident at the Polish Sejm, encouraged Catherine to try to handle her Polish crisis in the 1790s by pressuring the Uniate Church even more aggressively than she had at the time of the first partition.

In 1787, one year before the opening of the Sejm, Smohozhevs'kyi still tended the Uniates of Poland in the good graces of a benignly aloof government; he could boast of a great new church in Warsaw. In the same year, Lisovs'kyi, appointed to fill the Polatsk vacancy four years before, found himself happily favored by his Russian sovereign. It was the year of Catherine's magnificent Dnieper regatta procession to the Crimean peninsula.

Lisovs´kyi and Siestrzeńcewicz were also summoned to the
Crimea in June 1787, and while the latter was rewarded there
with a new Roman Catholic church—an ancient Greek temple
that the Muslims had used for baths—the former received for the
Uniates a mosque to be converted to Christian worship. In June
1788 the Propaganda Fide in Rome believed that Russian rule was
no imminent menace to the Uniate Church. On the contrary, after
the bestowal of the Crimean mosque, and with the outbreak of
a new Russian-Ottoman war, Rome entertained "the most flattering hopes, with the benediction of the Lord, for the further
propagation of Catholicism in those regions, should the outcome
of the war be favorable to Russia."[70] Here was a total reversal of
perspective from that of Catherine's first Russian-Ottoman war.
In 1774 Rome had been counting on a Turkish victory so that the
sultan might protect the Uniates from Russia.

It was the unsettling of the political status quo between
Poland and Russia after 1788 that consequently unsettled the
religious stability of the preceding years. When the Russian-
Ottoman war finally did end in 1791, there was little cause to
persist in the "flattering hopes" that Rome had once entertained.
In 1792 Russian armies were free to invade Poland, putting an
end to the Four-Year Sejm, and in 1793 Catherine, together with
Frederick William II, imposed upon the Commonwealth a second
partition. Thereby she significantly increased her population
of Uniate subjects, acquiring a large part of Ukraine, including
most of the metropolitan diocese. In a decree of 1794 Catherine
actually spoke of pursuing "the eradication of the Uniate faith"
but nevertheless styled the campaign as one of "exhortation" to
return to Orthodoxy.[71] Ludwig Pastor, in his classic *History of the
Popes*, basing his account on that of Pelesh, noted Catherine's
insincerity and flatly concluded: "Catherine II, the destruction
of Poland accomplished, prepared to deal the death-blow to the

---

70   *Acta S. C. de Propaganda Fide*, 5:156.

71   Skinner, *Western Front*, 203–5.

Greek Union, this being the second object of her Polish policy and one which she had pursued all along." Madariaga comments that "in common with most contemporary Orthodox officials and with subsequent Orthodox historians, Catherine regarded the Uniate religion as an unhappy marriage of the dogmas of one faith with the ritual of another, an artificial creation, specially invented to seduce the Orthodox population of Belarus from their allegiance to Moscow."[72] Certainly, Catherine was sensitive to the political implications of religious allegiance, and after the second partition she regarded with concern the increased number of her Uniate subjects. Barbara Skinner has observed that Catherine considered the conversion of the Uniates "not as conversion per se, but as an act of undoing the religious damage of Polish rule and reclaiming the historical religious tradition of Orthodoxy," and as a religious realization of the East Slavic unity achieved by the partitions. At the same time, Catherine's interest in Orthodoxy was stimulated earlier, in the 1780s, by the elaboration, together with Potemkin, of the so-called Greek Project for conquering Constantinople, the former capital of Orthodox Byzantium. Literary historian Andrei Zorin has noted that Russian state ideology in the late eighteenth century was accordingly inflected by religious concerns that played a part in Catherine's imperial perspective.[73]

Accordingly, in 1794 Russia inaugurated an Orthodox missionary campaign directed at the new Uniate populations. That same year witnessed the Kościuszko insurrection in Poland, the outbreak of full-scale revolutionary war against Russia. In fact, the Kościuszko insurrection began in March, while the missionary campaign opened with a great pastoral appeal in May—accompanied by Russian denunciations of the Uniates for participation in the insurrection. Five years before, the Uniates had been denounced in the Commonwealth for participating in seditious

---

72   Ludwig Pastor, *The History of the Popes*, vol. 39 (Pius VI), trans. E. F. Peeler (London, 1952), 172–73; Madariaga, *Russia in the Age of Catherine*, 514.

73   Skinner, *Western Front*, 200–1; Zorin, *By Fables Alone*, 24–60.

conspiracies against the Sejm, and now Russia, too, insisted on the significance of religious affiliation for political loyalty. In 1794 the violent disordering of Catherine's Polish policy coincided with the aggressive assault on the Uniates. In 1768 Catherine's military response to Polish political defiance in the Confederation of Bar had been accompanied by harassment of the Uniates of Ukraine, and in 1794 she acted similarly at the moment of the Kościuszko insurrection. Once again religious pressure was her response to political instability, but the lessons of the intervening generation, as well as the greater territorial rearrangements of the second and third partitions, ensured that this time the pressure would be more radically applied.

In 1793 Catherine consulted the Orthodox Synod concerning the Uniates, and the Synod in turn consulted the Greek churchman Evgenios Voulgaris. He had served in Russia since the 1770s, and now prepared a memorandum "On the Best Means for Reunification of the Uniates with the Orthodox Church." Voulgaris, in many ways a man of the Greek Enlightenment, rejected violence as a means of reunification, and emphasized instead exemplary pastoral appointments and a comprehensive system of religious education for "correct instruction in the faith." Historian Paschalis Kitromilides has further indicated the significance of Voulgaris, in Catherine's service, for helping to integrate Orthodoxy into an ideology of enlightened absolutism, encompassing the Greek Project, for the wider Orthodox world.[74] Though the Orthodox campaign against the Uniates in the 1790s would prove to be less pacific than Voulgaris envisioned, official interest in his ideas about "The Best Means for Reunification" suggests that Catherine herself may not yet have decided upon her means or her ends.

---

74   Paschalis Kitromilides, *Enlightenment and Revolution: The Making of Modern Greece* (Cambridge: Harvard University Press, 2013), 126-33; Stephen K. Batalden, *Catherine II's Greek Prelate: Eugenios Voulgaris in Russia, 1771-1806* (Boulder and New York, 1982), 85-87; Skinner, *Western Front*, 201-2.

At the head of the missionary campaign in 1794 stood Viktor Sadkovs´kyi, who had represented Orthodox interests within the Commonwealth since the first partition, initially as the chaplain of the Russian embassy in Warsaw, then as archimandrite of the monastery at Slutsk, and finally as Orthodox archbishop of Minsk. Sadkovs´kyi had recently been released from arrest in Poland, under suspicion of sedition since 1789, and now he aggressively made the case for Orthodox victimization in the Commonwealth. The commitment of the Russian state to Sadkovs´kyi was expressed in an annual fund of 20,000 rubles for his missionary work and the promise of cooperation from the Russian army.

In the inaugural pastoral appeal of 1794, Sadkovs´kyi lamented past persecution of the Orthodox in Poland, and called upon all those "whose grandparents, fathers, or themselves were brought by fraud or by fear from Orthodoxy to union with the Latins, to return without fear to the arms of the Orthodox Church."[75] This appeal was read in the Uniate churches of Catherine's new lands, and the conclusion made explicit the political concerns of the whole campaign.

> Arise, children of the Church, and find satisfaction in the freedom of the Orthodox confession that inspired your ancestors and many of yourselves. The persecution has ceased, the storms have subsided. Hurry into the arms of the Church, your mother, so that the peace of conscience may make you happy, so that you may proceed along the path of truth that leads us to grace and glory. And may each of you, according to his condition, besides avowing the truths of the Orthodox religion, also fulfill his duty of loyalty to the supreme ruler and the state.[76]

---

75   Likowski, *Geschichte des allmaeligen Verfalls*, 1:267; Ludomir Bieńkowski, "Organizacja Kościoła Wschodniego w Polsce," in Jerzy Kłoczowski, ed., *Kościół w Polsce*, vol. 2, *Wieki XVI–XVIII* (Cracow, 1970), 859.

76   Likowski, *Geschichte des allmaeligen Verfalls*, 1:268.

Twenty years before, it had been enough for Smohozhevs´kyi
and his clergy to render publicly their oath of loyalty to Catherine in the Polatsk cathedral. Now, a more modern conception of
political duties and loyalties required a more profound affirmation of loyalty from a more complete domain of the population.
Religious conversion was to be both proof and guarantee of the
change in sovereignty.

This radicalization of religious harassment was revealed
in the conduct of the campaign of 1794. At the time of the first
partition, Uniate priests in Ukraine had served as focal points for
Russian pressure; they were bullied, arrested, and replaced. Now,
when a team of Orthodox priests and Russian soldiers arrived
in a Uniate village, they assembled the entire community and
applied pressure to everyone. There was missionary preaching
followed by dark threats and even beatings in church. Above all,
there was an appeal for signatures, and conversion to Orthodoxy
was confirmed by the signing of individual names (or signing
crosses, for the illiterate). The standard document for signing
declared that "rejecting the non-Orthodox Uniate faith, we want
and desire to be in the confession and embrace of the holy Eastern
Orthodox Church"—with the document then notarized as having
been "signed in their own hand and of their own accord."[77] Such
collecting of witnessed signatures was persecution conceived in
a modern spirit, initiated in the culminating year of the French
revolutionary Terror, and appropriately aimed at terrorizing the
Uniate Church as an aggregation of individuals, not just as a
religious corporate structure. Furthermore, it was these signatures that provided the fig leaf of justification invoked by state
authority. According to the protests of Metropolitan Rostots´kyi:

> Wherever priests and people, in spite of threats and terrors, re-
> mained steadfast, then, even when they [the persecutors] had ob-
> tained only a few signatures from the community, they confiscated

---

77   Skinner, *Western Front*, 210.

the church with all its furnishings, took the whole village under
their spiritual administration and drove out the Uniate priests.[78]

Thus, the collection of signatures preceded the usurpation
of property and priesthood. Churches were appropriated either
by crude thuggery, with Orthodox missionaries climbing in the
windows, or by more refined legal harassment as foundation
papers were carefully examined for evidence of Orthodox possession as far back as the Union of 1596.

The great institutional blow to the Uniate Church was deliv-
ered by Catherine in 1795, just at the time of the third, final, and
complete partition of Poland. She dismissed the Uniate bishops
who now fell under her sovereignty, including the metropolitan,
and their dioceses, which since the previous year had been lo-
cally assaulted, were now effectively abolished by decree from
St. Petersburg: all the Uniates of the Russian Empire were to be
placed under the one remaining Uniate spiritual authority, the
archbishop of Polatsk. This was Lisovs´kyi, who had been chosen by Catherine herself after so much suspense in 1783, and
his preservation, indeed his aggrandizement, clearly explained
the dismissal of his colleagues. They were all the appointments
of Stanisław August, a king now forced into ignominious abdication and retirement himself; they were all subjects of the
Commonwealth, a state that no longer existed on the map of
Europe. Catherine's long cherished policy of diplomatic domination in Poland had failed absolutely, and she now faced the more
complex challenge of political annexation and administration.
The Kościuszko insurrection in 1794 gave some idea of how difficult and perilous this challenge might prove to be in an age of
increasingly emphatic national sentiment. Catherine responded
by targeting the Uniates and applying the now practiced techniques of enlightened absolutism—expropriating, consolidating,
pensioning, subordinating—the techniques of sovereign authority
in religious affairs. At the same time she sponsored a missionary

---

78   Likowski, *Geschichte des allmaeligen Verfalls*, 1:270–71.

campaign, conceived in an aggressively modern spirit, to meet the modern challenge of imperial integration. The relationship between Church and state would no longer provide the only political key to government in the region; Catherine had begun to recognize the political importance of the relationship between religious practice and cultural identity.

She died in 1796, with the ramifications of the abolition of Poland still unresolved, and with the missionary campaign against the Uniates still unabating. In nineteenth-century Catholic historiography, it was assumed that Catherine had always intended to destroy the Uniate Church, and the campaign of her last years was interpreted as positive proof of that intention, the ultimate revelation of her malevolence. The historian Likowski supposed that she would have eradicated the Union altogether in Russia, anticipating Nicholas by half a century, "if God had extended her life by several years."[79] By this interpretation, her death was nothing less than an instance of divine intervention. It is true that the succession of Paul brought a respite for the Uniates, but Catherine's deathbed intentions remain difficult to estimate. Such estimation ought to be based on the facts of the campaign of 1794–1796, but also on the whole record of her reign in Uniate affairs. An important aspect of the last campaign, in this regard, was the preservation of the archbishop of Polatsk when all the other bishops were being sent into forced retirement. At the same time, while missionary harassment was both intense and efficacious in the newly annexed lands of the second and third partitions, the Polatsk diocese remained relatively immune. This at least suggests that Catherine may not have been committed to the complete extermination of the Union.

In fact, her missionary intentions were focused on the newly acquired lands, and especially Ukraine. There the effects were devastating; the Uniates lost more than two thousand parishes, and were in many areas almost institutionally eliminated. The

---

79   Likowski, *Geschichte des allmaeligen Verfalls*, 1:282.

imbalance of the assault, however, the targeting in particular of the Uniates of Ukraine, suggested a government policy more subtle and specific than simple crusading. Catherine had unleashed an Orthodox campaign in Ukraine once before, between 1768 and 1775. At that time the religious pressure had ceased as soon as Catherine was satisfied with the outcome of the Polish Partition Sejm. Between 1794 and 1796 she applied the same pressure in the same place at the time of another partition crisis. As for the pensioning of the Uniate bishops, Catherine also had applied pressure at the episcopal level once before, between 1779 and 1783 when the archbishopric of Polatsk lay vacant, and finally she had named a new bishop after clearly establishing her own imperial authority in religious affairs.

Catherine's persecution of the Uniates in 1794 was the evolutionary product of a thirty-year reign. Interpreted in the light of her previous dealings with the Uniates, especially during the menacing interludes of 1768–1775 and 1779–1783, the final campaign of 1794–1796—with as many as 1.6 million converts to Orthodoxy reported—may well have been intended as an expression of political pressure and sovereign authority.[80] That her injuries to the Union were not irreversible was demonstrated by the reversal that soon followed under Paul. In December 1796 Rostots´kyi already was saluting Paul in St. Petersburg:

> The voice of your persecuted and oppressed subjects, great monarch, has reached the throne of your majesty and has been heard. You restore freedom and happiness to a people who were oppressed only because they honored God according to the faith of their fathers...King of kings, you saw our misery, and now you see our happiness bestowed upon us by a good monarch.[81]

---

80   Skinner, *Western Front*, 219.

81   *Akty izdavaemye Vilenskoiu arkheograficheskoiu kommissieiu*, 16:569.

Sadkovs´kyi in 1794 proposed to restore the Uniates to the fold of their Orthodox ancestors; Rostots´kyi in 1796 looked to the more recent past when he welcomed them back to the faith of their Uniate fathers. The reversal of policy was already under way as soon as Catherine died and Paul succeeded her. Rostots´kyi, in fact, came very close to openly denouncing Catherine for her oppression of the Uniates, something he could only dare to do when addressing the son who so strongly resented her. Paul reestablished the Uniate dioceses within the Russian Empire, as parishes returned to the Union.

In 1797 Lorenzo Litta, the last Warsaw nuncio, went to St. Petersburg as papal legate, and proceeded to negotiate the reestablishment of a Uniate hierarchy of three dioceses in the Russian Empire. These were no longer the remnants of old Polish dioceses, but a new hierarchy tailored to the new Russian borders. In 1797 Russia, Prussia, and Austria agreed by secret treaty "to abolish everything which could revive the memory of the existence of the Kingdom of Poland."[82] When Pope Pius VI ratified Litta's diocesan arrangements in 1798, he accepted at the same time the sovereignty of the Russian state over those former lands of the extinct Commonwealth. As political uncertainties were resolved, religious pressure was lifted.

In 1805 Rostots´kyi, "Metropolitan of Kyiv, Halych, and Rus´," the last metropolitan of Stanisław August, died in retirement in St. Petersburg. The dethroned king also had passed away in St. Petersburg, seven years before in 1798, and the Commonwealth itself was already ten years gone since 1795. In 1806 Tsar Alexander I reactivated the metropolitanate by appointing an active successor, but the post itself was really a new one, designated with a new title to erase any shadow of a connection to the old Commonwealth: "Metropolitan of the Uniate Church in Russia." Alexander chose Lisovs´kyi, Catherine's archbishop of Polatsk.

---

82   Norman Davies, *God's Playground: A History of Poland*, vol. 1 (1982; New York, 1984), 542.

In that same year, the Habsburg emperor Francis I approved the creation of another new metropolitanate for the Uniates of Austria. The post was entitled "Metropolitan of Halych," thus distinguishing Habsburg Galicia from the defunct Commonwealth, and the chosen churchman was Antin Anhelovych, who had once been Joseph's rector at the General Seminary in Lviv. Thus, in 1806 the Uniates of the Habsburg and Romanov territories faced the nineteenth century with two distinct hierarchies, each with a metropolitan of its own, both cut off from the old Commonwealth hierarchy that had constituted the Uniate Church for two hundred years. It was no coincidence that the new metropolitanates were assigned to clerics who made their careers in the 1780s: Lisovs´kyi, Catherine's man, and Anhelovych, Joseph's man. Enlightened absolutism had transformed the Uniate Church in Austria and in Russia, and, although the Uniate experience was notably dissimilar in those two states, in both cases relations between Church and state were reordered according to enlightened principles of authority. These institutional parallels left the Uniates of both territories far more susceptible to the power of their respective sovereigns. That power would be exercised very differently by the Habsburgs and the Romanovs in the nineteenth century. The former would sponsor a religious and cultural revival, while the latter would adopt a policy of persecution and demolition. These nineteenth-century divergences, however, should not retrospectively color the historical appreciation of the characteristic structural transformations imposed upon the Uniate Church by enlightened absolutism in the eighteenth century.

Part II. Ritual and Identity

For Love of the Jesuits

From November 1772 to January 1773, Smohozhevs´kyi was in St. Petersburg, courting his new sovereign and attempting to attain assurances of the security of his Uniate diocese of Polatsk, now incorporated into Catherine's empire. His conscientious courtiership allowed him not only to sample the artichokes and watermelons supplied to the imperial table, but also to make the acquaintance of the great ladies who attended the court of the tsarina. His sociability was sufficiently successful to attract a bevy of countesses from the grandest families—Golitsyn, Razumovskii, Naryshkin—to the liturgies that he celebrated in the Catholic church of St. Petersburg. He reported with satisfaction to Rome that these ladies "left convinced that there exists no essential difference between my masses and those of Russia." Afterwards, in conversation, he was repeatedly asked about different details of the ceremony—vestments, missals, bells, the Eucharist—and he replied, "joking with modesty," in such a way as to convince the ladies that any variations did not "damage the essence" of the Greek rite. After these replies, he reported to the Warsaw nuncio, all objections "vanished."[83] This report

---

83   Smogorzewski, *Epistolae*, 87–88.

made the demonstration in St. Petersburg into a double-edged declaration, teaching suspicious and curious Russians that the Uniate rite was reassuringly familiar, while at the same time reminding the Vatican that the Uniates were ritually distinct from Roman Catholics. From its creation in 1596, the mixed nature of the Union—combining Catholic authority and theology with an Orthodox clergy and ritual—was troubling to aggressive purists in both the Catholic and Orthodox camps. In 1772, the partition of Poland and aggrandizement of Russian power and influence made it all the more important that the Uniate Church unequivocally affirm its own mixed construction, as a condition of independent identity and survival. If such self-identification was first practiced in 1772 at the highest levels of the episcopal hierarchy—as in the case of Smohozhevs´kyi—over the next generation its urgency would be experienced at every level of the Uniate Church, in all its social contexts, as village communities were invited to choose their own priests and individual peasants were solicited for their signatures.

Smohozhevs´kyi in St. Petersburg was not always in female company. He often visited with three members—"learned and humane"—of the Orthodox Synod, to discuss privately the points of division between Orthodoxy and Catholicism, and even the possibilities of general reunion. These discussions were friendly even in disagreement, allowing for "intimate little disputes" (*famigliari disputarelle*). They culminated in a seven-hour informal symposium on issues of ritual and theology, with serious debate over the nature of the Eucharist. "Heated by such a long conversation," Smohozhevs´kyi had to take to his bed with fever for four days, "diverting" himself by reading Greek authorities on Eucharistic forms. Fully recovered and returned to society at the home of Count Chernyshev, he was provoked in company—by an outspoken Russian theologian—to pronounce publicly upon the possible union of the Churches. His listeners appeared "strongly surprised" to learn that "the pope seeks nothing but dogmatic Union, and, in the rest, regarding the sacred rites and truly pious and honest customs, as well as ecclesiastical liberty, he is accustomed without difficulty to condescend to the desires of nations (*alle brame delle Nazioni*)"—as demonstrated in the case of the Ruthenian Uniates themselves.[84] Again the declaration cut two ways, offering the Russian Empire the Uniate Church as a model of ecumenical unity, while informing Rome of the precise terms in which the Uniate archbishop would construe and defend the Catholicism of the Uniates.

The message to the Vatican was underlined by the extraordinary exclamation, addressed to the Warsaw nuncio Garampi, that followed at this point in the dispatch. For the "surprise" of the company, like the questions of the ladies after mass, confirmed for Smohozhevs´kyi that in the Russian Empire there prevailed the most damaging misimpressions of the Uniate compromise. Yet he did not blame either St. Petersburg or Orthodoxy:

> Ah! my Reverend Monsignor, now I understand how much has been contributed to the stubbornness (*cocciutaggine*) of the Orthodox (*disuniti*), and to the present disasters of Poland, by that selfish (*interessato*) zeal of the Jesuit fathers, and also of some Latin bishops, exercised most damagingly for more than a hundred years, to render despised (*vilipeso*), ridiculous, and also abhorred the sacred rite of these Uniates, in order to occupy the property of their churches, to transfer so many villages, so many cities, and so many noble families of the Greek Catholic rite to the Latin rite, having in this manner debilitated the Church and the condition of the Uniates, and reinforced that of the Orthodox.[85]

In short, for the suspicion he encountered in St. Petersburg as a Uniate in 1772, he blamed a long history of Roman Catholic contempt and despoliation in Poland, especially by the Jesuits. The Uniate Church, from its founding in 1596, depended upon a

---

84   Smogorzewski, *Epistolae*, 87–89.

85   Smogorzewski, *Epistolae*, 89.

negotiated compromise between Orthodoxy and Catholicism, and that balance seemed more urgently threatened by Latin forces in Poland right up until 1772. Suspicion of Rome lingered through the next generation, and even acquired additional force from the need to demonstrate in the Russian Empire, as Smohozhevs´kyi did, that the Uniates preserved their Greek rites.

Smohozhevs´kyi was a carefully political prelate, and just as he underplayed any anxiety about Russian Orthodoxy while at the court of Catherine, so he could hardly denounce Roman Catholicism without qualification in a report to the Warsaw nunciature for relay to the Vatican. The blaming of the Jesuits was the solution to this political awkwardness, and they came to serve as a focus for Uniate resentment against the high-handedness of Roman Catholic sponsorship. There was a certain historical injustice in this, for it was a sixteenth-century Jesuit, Antonio Possevino, who played a leading role in the creation of the Uniate Church, while seventeenth-century Jesuits, as in the case of the Chinese rites, had advocated precisely the sort of open construction of Catholicism that Smohozhevs´kyi described in St. Petersburg as the key to religious union. The Jesuits in the eighteenth century, however, were natural scapegoats, denounced across Europe in a spirit of both Jansenism and Enlightenment, and finally abolished as an order by the Vatican itself in July 1773, the very same month that Smohozhevs´kyi wrote his report on the visit to St. Petersburg. In 1770 he already complained from Polatsk that he could devote more time to the defense of the Uniates, "if I were not disquieted and persecuted by the Jesuits of this College." In 1772 he protested against "Jesuitical usurpations and persecutions," warning Rome that "for love of the Jesuits it is not fitting to keep in ignorance the secular clergy of the Uniates, nor to leave open the door to transit *ex Ritu ad Ritum*, and now what use can I have from my poor and ignorant priests?"[86] Thus, the Jesuits represented that privileged part of Roman Catholicism,

---

86   Smogorzewski, *Epistolae*, 59, 69.

privileged in property and in education, that underlined by contrast the poverty and ignorance of the Uniate clergy. At the same time, their worldly advantages made them appear as religious predators, undermining the Uniate Church by drawing off its members in transit to the Roman rite.

After the suppression of the Jesuits by the Vatican, they continued to exist insubordinately in Russia with the encouragement of Catherine, and Smohozhevs´kyi gave emphatic expression to his resentment in denunciations to Rome. The Jesuits had been ordered to divest themselves of their "habits," the distinctive costumes of their order: "but I believe that changing habit will not change the hide—on the contrary, Jesuitism hidden and everywhere dispersed will be dangerous, so it will be necessary to see to it that no two of these Venerable Members should ever find themselves together in the same place." Such paranoia was consistent with the most conventional eighteenth-century anticlerical myths of Jesuit plotting and conspiracy. Indeed, Jesuit insubordination in the face of the suppression of the society highlighted the crucial and defining issue of Catholicism for the Uniates: their own hierarchical subordination to the pope, in spite of their un-Roman rites. Smohozhevs´kyi took satisfaction in reporting himself "horrified" to hear an angry Jesuit theologian "vomiting" his opinion, regarding the suppression of his order, that "Luther left the Roman Church for less reason."[87] By 1774 the Uniate churchman achieved an even cruder intensity of expression, denouncing the supreme "bestiality" of Jesuit writings (*bestialissime irriflessioni*), at which point his outrage almost seemed to partake of the anticlerical fervor so favored by the age of Enlightenment. That same year, in the house of a Polish woman from a family with Jesuit connections (she herself rather crudely characterized as *grandissima Gesuitessa*), Smohozhevs´kyi encountered a "pseudo-Jesuit" (*Gesuitino*) and warned him against trying to celebrate any masses in Uniate churches.

---

87   Smogorzewski, *Epistolae*, 103–5.

The *Gesuitino* "ran" to complain to his "pseudo-Rector" (*Rettorone*), and Smohozhevs´kyi feared they would attack him at court in Warsaw.[88] Evidently, his fear was not so great, or he would not have spoken so plainly—in the mocking tones of *Gesuitino* and *Rettorone*—but the fury of his comments on the Jesuits during these years of their misfortune suggested a spiritual liberation from past intimidations.

Such seemingly gratuitous vehemence must be taken as an important symptomatic manifestation of the Uniate hierarchical mentality in the 1770s. These odd outbursts reflected more than resentment about the Jesuits preying upon the Uniate Church or about the symbolic juxtaposition of the privileged and underprivileged within the Catholic world. Anger at the Jesuits reflected a whole historical perspective on the purpose and direction of the Uniate Church, from its foundation in 1596 to its new exigencies after 1772. The date of the Union of Brest in 1596 lends itself to alternative interpretations. Was the Union a triumph of the Counter-Reformation, ten years after the failure of the Spanish Armada, a Jesuit conquest in Eastern Europe whereby millions were converted from Orthodoxy to Catholicism? Or was it a late Renaissance compromise, in the same spirit of religious conciliation that characterized the contemporary reigns of Tudor Queen Elizabeth I in England and Habsburg Emperor Rudolf II in Prague? The research of David Frick suggests that in the urban context of seventeenth-century Vilnius it was possible for the Uniates to negotiate neighborly patterns of social and cultural coexistence with other Christian communities of the city.[89]

Smohozhevs´kyi in St. Petersburg in the late eighteenth century clearly considered it an important point—of external policy toward state authority and of religious identity within

---

88   Smogorzewski, *Epistolae*, 147.

89   David Frick, *Kith, Kin, and Neighbors: Communities and Confessions in Seventeenth-Century Wilno* (Ithaca: Cornell University Press, 2013), 77–98 and 117–72.

the Church—to insist on a spirit of compromise presiding over the foundation and development of the Union. It was thus that he himself held forth upon the nature of religious union, concluding with historical references that revealed his interest in the Renaissance. The pope, he explained at the home of Chernyshev, was "accustomed without difficulty to condescend to the desires of nations, just as Eugenius IV condescended to the Greek propositions at the Council of Florence, and Clement VIII to the demands of the Ruthenians of Poland."[90] Thus, linking the reigns of Eugenius IV (1431–1447) and Clement VIII (1592–1605), and comparing the Council of Florence (1439) with the Union of Brest (1596), the eighteenth-century archbishop implicitly assigned the creation of the Uniate Church to an age of Renaissance union and compromise.

The Jesuits, with their Ignatian religious militancy, with their reputation for cleverness and machination, represented for Smohozhevsʹkyi the alternative and false interpretation of the Union in terms of the Counter-Reformation. If the Union was no sincere compromise, but a simple victory for Catholicism, then the Rusʹ populations had fallen for a Jesuit trick and changed their religion solely to serve the purpose of Counter-Reformation self-aggrandizement. In fact, this was the conventional Russian and Orthodox perspective on the Union—that it was created, in Catherine's words, "by various tricks of the Catholic clergy"—and therefore Smohozhevsʹkyi encountered Russian "surprise" when he explained the true nature of his Church. He himself deeply resented what he saw as Jesuit contempt for the Uniates, and he made it his business in the Russian Empire to refute that Jesuit perspective on the Union and Jesuit preying upon Uniate properties and populations. That contempt and those appropriations were the signs of an interpretation of the whole Union that Smohozhevs'kyi would not accept and sought to refute.

---

90   Frick, *Kith, Kin, and Neighbors,* 89; see also Gudziak, *Crisis and Reform,* 77–88, 245–55.

This historical concern was all the more relevant in the late eighteenth century, because the proper work of the Counter-Reformation remained still to be completed in the age of Enlightenment. Jean Delumeau has argued that the fundamental achievement of the Counter-Reformation in Western Europe was the "Christianization" of a clergy that previously showed a rather weak standard of piety and dedication, so that priests might in turn Christianize a hitherto deeply superstitious and ignorant population.[91] The "ignorance" that Smohozhevs´kyi frankly noted in his own parish clergy called for Christian education, so that the likewise ignorant peasant laity might also achieve that level of religious identity necessary to the survival of the Uniate Church. He did not hesitate to propose that confiscated properties of the suppressed Jesuits should fund the education of the Uniate clergy: "Good God, such properties from their most antique foundations should belong to my clergy, needful of education more than anything else, the security of the Catholic religion depending upon this."[92]

His denunciations of the Jesuits, even his interest in confiscations, allowed the archbishop's religious program to be curiously conditioned by eighteenth-century enlightened values. Even his concern about ignorance and education, combined as it was with hostility to the Jesuits, involved the spirit of both Counter-Reformation and Enlightenment. When he left Russia in 1780 to bring those same values to Poland as the metropolitan, he reminded Catherine of his educational and economic enterprises as evidence of his good service to her. Above all, it was his unrelenting attitude toward the Jesuits that allowed him to make the idea of religious union into an ideological connection between Renaissance and Enlightenment, effacing or revising the values of the problematic Counter-Reformation. His spirited speech, on behalf of a union that would allow "ecclesiastical liberty" to the

---

91   Jean Delumeau, *Catholicism between Luther and Voltaire: A New View of the Counter-Reformation*, trans. Jeremy Moiser (1971; London, 1977), 175–202.

92   Smogorzewski, *Epistolae*, 115.

"desires of nations," took on some of the rhetorical coloring of Lessing or Voltaire. After all, his hyperbolic hatred of the Jesuits in itself brought the archbishop of Polatsk into peculiar alignment with the patriarch of Ferney. By his rejection of the Jesuits and his celebration of their suppression, Smohozhevs'kyi signaled a certain modernity of purpose, which may be observed at every level and location of the Uniate Church during the last decades of the eighteenth century. With the passing of the ancien régime, a specifically Uniate identity was cultivated in ritual and disseminated through education, to adapt an early modern religious experiment to forms and standards of piety consistent with the conditions of modern society.

Insolent and Malignant Transit

In 1773, at the height of his outrage against the Jesuits, Smohozhevs'kyi also found energy to denounce the activities of certain local Carmelites who were converting Uniates within his diocese to Roman Catholicism. He declared himself "scandalized by these Carmelite fathers, discalced but rich enough"—thus sounding the note of resentment against privilege—and lamented that "they weaken the Church of the Uniates, inflame the Orthodox, and scandalize even the Jews."[93] The issue of Uniate "transit" to Roman Catholicism was one that came up as well with regard to the Jesuits, not just as a contemporary problem of Uniates passing *ex Ritu ad Ritum*, but also as an historical reflection upon the seventeenth-century Polish assimilation of the Rus´ nobility—"so many noble families of the Greek Catholic rite"—with Jesuit schools exercising a certain cultural magnetism upon Uniate boys. It was striking that the Uniate Church in 1773 should have interested itself so acutely in the scandal of "transit" to Roman Catholicism at precisely the time that Russian armies in Ukraine facilitated widespread and ongoing "apostasy" to

---

93   Smogorzewski, *Epistolae*, 99.

Orthodoxy. In fact, these issues were perceived as interlocking parts of the same problem, inasmuch as Roman Catholic contempt bred Orthodox contempt, and any pressure from the Roman side was dangerously inflammatory in Russia. For Smohozhevs´kyi in St. Petersburg, the key to preserving the Union within an Orthodox state was to demonstrate the sincerity of its founding compromise. Such demonstration was not simply political in purpose, for compromise was also the key to internal viability and vitality, enabling the Uniate Church to satisfy the ritual and spiritual concerns of its members.

Smohozhevs´kyi had studied in Rome as a young man from 1734 to 1740, and it was there that he acquired not only his richly expressive command of Italian, but also the learned expertise to pronounce upon the fateful importance of the transit issue for the Uniates:

> During the time of my stay in Rome, I digested all the material on transit, and I am absolutely persuaded that the ruin of the Catholic religion here continues as the consequence of such insolent and malignant transit. I have spoken and written enough about this, but the singularly Jesuitical arrogance, by means of calumny, has impeded the holy effects of the apostolic prohibition established even in the years 1624, 1636, and 1742. Now is the time that the Holy See should show the world that in fact it desires the integrity of the Greek Catholic rite, that it censures, abhors, and condemns whoever weakens it, derides it, discourages it, and finally whoever, with a thousand arts, under the pretext of sanctity, seeks to extinguish it.[94]

The specific transgressions of the Carmelites were rhetorically absorbed into the more general malignancy of Jesuitical arrogance, as Smohozhevs´kyi called upon Rome to protect the Uniates by complementing the suppression of the Jesuits with a prohibition

---

94   Smogorzewski, *Epistolae*, 99.

against transit. In fact, he managed to obtain at this time the full support of Rome for that prohibition, achieving for his diocese within the Russian Empire that affirmation of Uniate distinctness that was withheld through two centuries in the Commonwealth.

In 1624, right after the Orthodox lynching in 1623 of the Uniate bishop of Polatsk, St. Josaphat Kuntsevych, Pope Urban VIII issued a decree against the transit of Uniates to Roman Catholicism. The Roman forces of influence around King Sigismund III, however, managed to obstruct the publication of the decree in Poland, and attrition among the Uniate nobility continued apace. There was a renewed interest in this issue in the middle of the eighteenth century, in the aftermath of the papal bull of 1742 "Etsi pastoralis," addressed to the Uniate Greeks of Sicily and Calabria. The bull was understood to attribute "precedence" (*praestantia*) to Roman Catholicism over the Greek rite, provoking concern among Uniates as far afield as Poland. In 1744 Pope Benedict XIV sent a message to the Warsaw nuncio on the subject of transit; the Jesuits of Poland were to be reminded that Rome did not approve of encouraging Uniates to embrace the Latin rite.[95] The Roman Catholic and Uniate hierarchies were polarized through the following decade over "Etsi pastoralis" and the transit issue, with the Uniate bishops gathering at Dubno in 1745, the Latin bishops at Hrodna (Grodno) in 1752, and the Uniates again at Vilnius in 1753. In 1752 Pope Benedict XIV queried the king of Poland, Augustus III, on the issue of transit, but the king preferred not to declare himself, and therefore eventually declined to involve the state in this Church affair. In 1755 the pope himself, in the constitution "Allatae sunt," expressed a commitment to the preservation of Oriental rites within the Roman Catholic Church, and a concomitant opposition to transit, but this could not be enforced in Poland without the support of the state and against the opposition of the Latin bishops.

---

95   Korczok, *Griechisch-katholische Kirche*, 87–93.

The controversy reached such a pitch in the 1750s that the Roman Catholic bishop of Przemyśl, Wacław Sierakowski, did not hesitate to turn the tables in a sensational fashion with a denunciation of Uniate priests who somehow surreptitiously baptized Roman Catholic children to force them into the Greek rite.[96] Uniate countercharges were sometimes of a similar nature, especially with regard to the influences exercised upon young pupils in Jesuit schools. The level of terror and malice that emerged when the transit issue became one of protecting children from abduction and seduction, suggests that the polarization of Roman Catholics against Uniates in early modern Poland could feed upon social tensions more often associated with superstitious anxiety about Jews or Roma. In fact, a Jewish ritual murder case—for the alleged murder of a Christian child—was prosecuted in 1753 in Zhytomyr in the Commonwealth.

The fever pitch of charges and countercharges between Uniates and Roman Catholics over "transit" in the 1750s oddly anticipated the intensely mutual recriminations over "apostasy" between Uniates and Orthodox in the 1760s. It was this context that explained how Smohozhevs´kyi could enter Catherine's empire in 1772, still worried that Roman Catholics were plotting to "ruin" and "extinguish" the Union through transit. For Uniate survival over the past generation had depended upon a two-front struggle to define its identity and preserve its numbers against the aggressive intentions of both Polish Roman Catholicism and Russian Orthodoxy.

In 1773, the Basilians of Polatsk registered the news from Warsaw of the humiliating treaties of partition, which separated Polatsk from Poland and confirmed its new place in the Russian Empire. Under these unprecedented and unsettling circumstances the monks examined their own Uniate identity in recalling the story of a teenage novice, Adam Miszun, who had to defend his vocation against the objections of his parents:

---

96   Korczok, *Griechisch-katholische Kirche*, 103n6.

The mother repeatedly said to her son, "Adalku, Adalku, don't you remember when you were little and cried in your cradle, and I went to you, by day and also by night, and now you have forgotten your mother, so that my tears don't move you." The son replied: "When I was little, I cried because I was stupid, but now you have sense but you cry without reason." And the Father remonstrated with his son: "Adalku, to whom will I leave my fortune, my money, et cetera." The son replied: "There is my younger brother, there is my sister." The mother again applied herself to other persuasions saying, "Adalku, what do you gain by becoming a Ruthene (*co tobie potym że zostaniesz rusinem*) and wearing a rustic cloak (*siermięga*) like a peasant." The son replied: "That doesn't matter at all, that I will be a Ruthene, because a Ruthene is just as good as a Roman."[97]

In 1773, stranded in the Russian Empire, the Uniates needed to affirm their identity by rejecting absolutely the presumptuous claims of Roman precedence.

Smohozhevs´kyi in 1773 was reflecting upon the seductive persuasions of transit to Roman Catholicism. It seemed altogether fitting that Clement XIV, the pope who abolished the Jesuits, should also at long last bring about the full formal publication of the Vatican's prohibition against transit. Thus Smohozhevs´kyi appealed from Polatsk in October 1773:

I know for sure that the Jesuits, unable to increase in Poland except upon the ruins of the Uniates, therefore made Urban VIII, of immortal memory, fear that the publication of the prohibition against transit would not be permitted by King Sigismund III. I know also, that in spite of these oppositions extorted by false supposition, the Apostolic See in the year 1636 validly decreed "not to have rescinded the decree of His Holiness" with which Urban VIII in the year 1624, under the gravest pains, forbade any transit by the Uniates without special dispensation of the Apos-

97 *Arkheograficheskii sbornik*, 10:375–76.

tolic See. The affair was decided, and the death of the great Pope
Benedict XIV impeded its publication. Divine Providence has left
it to the present Supreme Pastor, born and elevated to overcome
the greatest difficulties, and to unravel the truth from the pretexts,
that his paternal feelings should move him to act that the above
decree be finally notified to the bishops, the priests, and to the monastic communities in the former and modern dominion of Poland,
with precise orders never again on this point to stir up the poor
Ruthenian Uniates, afflicted from all sides, and more attached than
anyone else to the Holy Religion, the Apostolic See, and the Vicar
of Christendom.[98]

In fact, Clement XIV acceded to the petition from Polatsk, after
more than a century of papal hesitation, partly because the new
situation of the diocese in the Russian Empire, after the partition,
meant that transit to the Latin rite had now become politically
problematic.

One year later, in October 1774, Smohozhevsʹkyi finally received the long-awaited word from the prefect of the Propaganda
Fide and replied with gratitude: "I have never in my life had a
sweeter moment than that in which I received from Monsignor
Nuncio of Poland the most precious lines with which Your Em-
inence favored me on 16 July and accompanied by the most
clement brief of Our Lord, truly glorious and eternally adorable
hierarch of the Church of Christ."[99] Between the posting in July
and delivery in October, however, Clement XIV, that "adorable
hierarch," had died on 22 September, amid rumors that he was
poisoned by the Jesuits for his role in their suppression.

The Uniates of Belarus could hardly have loomed large for
the dying pope as he looked back upon his traumatic reign. In
Polatsk, however, his attention to transit was sweet indeed, as
an affirmation too long deferred through the history of early
modern Poland. It enabled Smohozhevsʹkyi and his successors

---

98   Smogorzewski, *Epistolae*, 106–7.

99   Smogorzewski, *Epistolae*, 147.

to turn their full attention to the problems of survival in an Orthodox state, though they were never able to discount altogether the possibility of danger from the Latin quarter. The precedent of confirming the prohibition against transit was important in itself, and it would be extended to the Habsburg monarchy in 1777 with the support of Maria Theresa. In 1778 the Propaganda Fide was still debating whether the confirmation of prohibition, issued for the Uniate Church in the Russian Empire, might be extended to what remained of Poland.[100] Smohozhevs′kyi in 1774 cherished that confirmation, not so much as an obstacle to defections as a declaration of identity and clarification of history. He rejoiced that now at last, "everyone, of whatever state and confession, will have to be fully convinced about the calumny, malignantly disseminated since 1596 and obstinately believed, that the Apostolic See, in desiring and promoting the ecclesiastical Union of the Ruthenians, never had anything else in mind but the weakening and then the extinction of their rites."[101] He had made this same point, regarding the sincerity of the Union, in dealing diplomatically with his hosts in St. Petersburg the year before, and it was also this clarification, beyond its diplomatic significance at court, which made the Union into something for the Uniates worth fighting to save.

The most likely Latin predator upon the Uniates of Belarus was none other than Siestrzeńcewicz, Catherine's highly favored Roman Catholic bishop at Mahilioŭ (Mogilev), who caused such embarrassment to Rome by protecting the Jesuits in the Russian Empire. In 1774 he was on his way home from St. Petersburg to Mahilioŭ, and stopped at Polatsk to visit Smohozhevs′kyi for half an hour. Siestrzeńcewicz ominously confided that in St. Petersburg people spoke of forcing the Uniates into Orthodoxy after the death of Smohozhevs′kyi, but also insisted, in apparent contradiction to this intention, that he himself had the

---

100 *Acta S. C. de Propaganda Fide*, 5:102.

101 Smogorzewski, *Epistolae*, 148.

government's permission to bring the Uniates over to the Latin rite. Smohozhevs´kyi believed in the Latin menace more readily than the Orthodox one, and immediately suspected some sort of Jesuit maneuver (*qualche politica de' Gesuiti*). He was confident that the government in St. Petersburg would respect the Uniates as long as the Roman Catholic clergy did not proselytize among them. Above all, he reported his concern that Siestrzeńcewicz was influencing that government against the urgently requested Vatican confirmation of the transit prohibition. "Eh!" exclaimed the Uniate archbishop of Polatsk with outrage against the nearby Roman Catholic bishop of Mahilioŭ, "let him exercise his zeal in the conversion of those who are not Catholic, and leave in peace the Uniates, faithful to Christ and to his Vicar, the Roman Pope." When the Vatican confirmation finally came, Siestrzeńcewicz was predictably obstructive about registering, publicizing, and communicating it to his clergy, revealing his dedication, according to Smohozhevs´kyi in 1775, to "the ulterior destruction of the Uniates."[102] The role of Siestrzeńcewicz as Latin nemesis of the Uniates in Russian Poland was paralleled by that of Sierakowski, Roman Catholic archbishop of Lviv, in Austrian Poland. As the bishop of Chełm in Poland in the 1750s he had made inflammatory accusations about the Uniate menace to Roman Catholic children, and in the 1770s, promoted to the archbishopric at Lviv, he used his influence in Vienna and throughout Galicia against the Uniates.

It was in Belarus, however, that Uniate transit to Roman Catholicism actually became a significant social reality, not just a symbolic issue of Vatican affirmation. During the four years from 1779 to 1783, when Catherine declined to fill the vacancy at Polatsk left by Smohozhevs´kyi's promotion to the metropolitanate, when Uniates were encouraged to choose freely "whatever priest the community desires," even the commitment of the Propaganda Fide in Rome was not enough to prevent some passage to the Latin rite as well as to Orthodoxy. One of the three

---

102   Smogorzewski, *Epistolae*, 115, 173.

members of the governing consistory, Innokentii Malynovs'kyi (Innocenty Malinowski), wondered whether it would be better to try to convert the whole diocese to the Latin rite as a refuge from Orthodoxy. In fact, Siestrzeńcewicz was conducting an active campaign of Roman Catholic proselytism during these years, welcoming thousands of Uniates, and the nineteenth-century historian Likowski vindicated this activity: "However much we may personally wish well to the Ruthenian Uniate Church, in the case of a Uniate who had only the choice between schism and the Latin rite we would without hesitation advise him to join the Latin Church."[103] An eighteenth-century Uniate churchman like Smohozhevs'kyi, however, refused to see the alternatives so starkly, and in fact three-quarters of the Uniate population in Belarus remained constant through these years. From within the Uniate hierarchy, the predations of Siestrzeńcewicz, Roman Catholic bishop of Mahilioŭ, as much as those of Heorhii Konys'kyi (Georgii Konisskii), Orthodox bishop of Mahilioŭ, appeared entirely deleterious. Records from the diocese of Chełm suggest the active nature of Roman Catholic efforts, for when Uniates in transit stated their reasons for changing rites, most spoke of receiving "advice" from Latin priests, especially Piarists and Jesuits.[104]

Smohozhevs'kyi believed after the partition that the prohibition of transit to Roman Catholicism was the best guarantee against provoking the aggressive intentions of Russian Orthodoxy. His reasoning was dramatically confirmed in 1786 in Poland, where he himself then presided as metropolitan. In that year, while the Sejm was meeting in Warsaw, an anonymous appeal to the Polish representatives was published, calling upon them to abolish by law the Uniate Church and incorporate its members into Roman Catholicism. The author cited pastoral reasons, alleging the ignorance and immorality of the Uniate clergy, and especially economic reasons—for the different religious holidays

---

103 Likowski, *Geschichte des allmaeligen Verfalls*, 1:204–5.

104 Madey, *Kirche zwischen Ost und West*, 122.

of the Latin and Uniate rites complicated economic life wherever the populations coincided.[105] Such an appeal to standards of education and economy appeared to be motivated by social values of the Enlightenment, all the more so in the presumptuously Josephinist suggestion that the Sejm should have any power at all to legislate, or even propose, such a course.

The only consequence of this anonymous piece of provocation was a magnificent propagandistic opportunity for the Orthodox bishop Konys´kyi, which he exploited in a powerful open letter to the Uniate bishops of the Commonwealth. His was precisely that calumny that Smohozhevs´kyi had fought to refute—that the Union was a mere trick, and that the Roman Catholics of Poland had long intended to extinguish the Greek rite of the Uniates. No less interested in the history of the Union than Smohozhevs´kyi himself, Konys´kyi recounted that at the Sejm of 1717, seventy years earlier, there also had been advocates for an assault on the Uniate Church. The Silent Sejm of 1717 had consummated the triumph of Peter I over the Commonwealth, and then, too, Polish fear of Russia had engendered suspicion of the Uniates. Now, in 1786, Konys´kyi claimed to summarize the Polish proposals of 1717: to speak with contempt of Uniate religious practice, to deny the Uniates education and give them uneducated priests and bishops, to subordinate Uniate bishops to Latin bishops, to conspire with Jews to displace Uniates from the towns and reduce them to feudal dependence. Konys´kyi then appealed to the Uniates from the perspective of 1786: "Now you say yourselves, whether everything contained in the project was not carried out in the following years right up to the present moment."[106] By the same token, the project of 1786 for the abolition of the Uniate Church could not be disregarded as the idle thoughts of an anonymous crank, but had to be studied instead as seriously programmatic.

_____

105 Likowski, *Geschichte des allmaeligen Verfalls*, 1:243.
106 Likowski, *Geschichte des allmaeligen Verfalls*, 1:246.

With scathing sarcasm Konys´kyi warned the Uniates against any religious union that was sponsored in Rome and consummated in Poland:

> Look at the beautiful and tempting example for the Greeks, to
> bring about union with the Roman Church! For Ruthenia a very
> appealing union of the Uniate Ruthenian with the Roman clergy in
> all liberties and privileges! A truly apostolic method and manner
> for spreading the Catholic faith, when by such measures one trans-
> forms the Ruthenian Catholics into Roman Catholics![107]

It was to undermine precisely such charges as these that Smohozhevs´kyi had sought to demonstrate the sincerity of the Union. Now Konys´kyi appealed to Smohozhevs´kyi himself, "reverend metropolitan," and his bishops, taunting them: "You flattered yourselves with the conviction that you were the true image of the original Greek Catholic Church, through the inseparable bond of faith and Christian love united with the Roman Catholic Church and amalgamated into one essence—look how your Roman Catholic brothers think about dealing with you." Konys´kyi assured the Uniates that neither the Roman pope, nor the Polish king, whatever their intentions, were powerful enough to protect the Uniate Church from destruction, and urged them to consider instead the protection of "the invincible empress of Russia." In Konys´kyi's view, this represented the only real road to religious union: "When you have laid aside the imaginary prejudice and antipathy against the Orthodox implanted by your annihilators, then you may be an instrument and fortunate means toward the encouragement of unity and of that union which rests upon the love and peace of Christ."[108] There was a certain convergence of discourse between Konys´kyi and Smohozhevs´kyi, as they addressed the same historical and theological issues with even

---

107   Likowski, *Geschichte des allmaeligen Verfalls*, 1:246.
108   Likowski, *Geschichte des allmaeligen Verfalls*, 1:247–48.

a measure of agreement in substance, but yet with that illusively unmeasurable gap in perspective that totally inverted each other's messages. They contested the contemporary identity of the Uniate Church according to their different confessional perspectives, by interpretively reviewing and revising the history of the Union.

According to the Custom of the Oriental Church

Konys´kyi's sarcastic tribute to the "union of the Uniate Ruthenian with the Roman clergy in all liberties and privileges" played upon longstanding tensions over a perceived inequality of rites. Papal rulings of the early seventeenth century protected the Uniate Church by guaranteeing its equality with the Roman Catholic Church in Poland, culminating in the 1643 declaration of the Propaganda Fide that "Ruthenian ecclesiastics should enjoy the same canonical privileges, immunities, and liberties as the Latin ecclesiastics." Yet, already in 1643 and 1644, Roman Catholic synods in Poland were revising the pronouncements of Rome, and whittling away at the supposed equality of rites. Latin priests were forbidden to celebrate mass in Uniate churches or to make their confessions to Uniate priests, while Uniate bishops were spitefully denied the title of "Illustrissimus."[109] Roman Catholic pretensions in Poland acquired new energy in the eighteenth century when in 1742 "Etsi pastoralis" seemed to assign precedence to the Latin Church in Sicily and Calabria. The Latin bishops in Poland laid claim to hierarchical superiority over the Uniate episcopate. In 1784, when Smohozhevs´kyi as metropolitan sought a suffragan bishop to assist him in the pastoral care of his vast diocese in Ukraine while he attended to politics in Warsaw, he warned the Vatican that the promotion would have to be handled with the utmost discretion: "so as not to alarm the Latin bishops, always jealous (sempre gelosi) of whatever advance in the Ruthenian

---

109   Korczok, Griechisch-katholische Kirche, 82–83.

clergy."[110] Not until 1792 at the Four-Year Sejm, with the Commonwealth on the brink of extinction, was the Uniate metropolitan Rostots´kyi brought into the Senate as a gesture toward the long obstructed equality of rites.

The Uniates of Poland, after two centuries of putting up with second-class status, were targeted by Konys´kyi as potentially malcontent, but this same issue of equality operated quite differently in Russian Poland and Austrian Poland after 1772. In the Russian Empire it was less important, for neither Catholic rite could enjoy the privileges of dominance in an Orthodox state. In Austrian Poland, on the other hand, where the Habsburgs had neither personal nor historical commitments to the disputation of privileges and rites within the early modern Commonwealth, the partition virtually reestablished the Uniate Church upon a new foundation of guarantees. In 1774 Maria Theresa officially ordered the Roman Catholic bishops of Galicia to instill in their clergies a spirit of "love and friendship" toward the Uniates.[111] That such love had to be imperially commanded was strongly suggestive of its absence hitherto. The Roman insinuations of Sierakowski, who traveled from Lviv to Vienna to urge upon the empress the attractions of *praestantia* and transit, were countered by the presence of the Uniate priest Ivan Huts´ (Huc), sent by Sheptyts´kyi from Lviv to Vienna to act for ten years as a sort of Uniate ambassador to the Habsburg capital.

In 1782 Joseph II further elaborated upon the principles of equality governing the relations of the different Catholic rites in Galicia. He took up the "love" motif suggested by his mother in 1774, and developed it into an enlightened allegory of religious coexistence:

> Since in Galicia the Catholic religion consists of three rites, namely the Latin, the Greek Uniate, and the Armenian Uniate, it is especial-

---

110 Smogorzewski, *Epistolae*, 353.

111 Korczok, *Griechisch-katholische Kirche*, 28.

ly important to see to it that these three daughters of one mother
should live in sisterly love, and among the peoples as well as
among the clergies of these confessions all discord is to be avoided. All three rites must be maintained in the same regard and no
one rite permitted to take precedence over both others, which are
just as venerable. All religious disputes between these three united
religions or contempt for their customs of worship and priests are
to be carefully avoided.[112]

Maria Theresa's ten surviving children included five daughters, so
Joseph knew something of the intricacies of sisterly coexistence
in family life. The allegory of the rites as three equal sisters was
even suggestive of Gotthold Ephraim Lessing's parable of the
three brothers and their three identical rings of religious truth in
Nathan the Wise, the enlightened drama of 1779. Though many of
Joseph's laws and principles were reconsidered after his death, his
brother Leopold II specifically confirmed the equality of Catholic
rites in Galicia in 1790, the year of his succession.

When Maria Theresa commanded love of the Uniates in 1774,
the same directive also insisted upon certain significant points
of terminology. The term "Greek Uniate" was to be dropped in
favor of "Greek Catholic," so that the Latin Church could not dis-
dain the rite as less than fully Catholic. Also, at the suggestion
of Sheptyts´kyi, other pejorative designations were forbidden: a
Uniate priest was not to be called *pop* (the Polish term used for
an Orthodox priest), and Uniate churches were not to be referred
to as "synagogues."[113] These were distinctions intended to allow
the Uniates equal dignity with the Roman Catholics, but at the
same time they were inevitably also interpretations of the Union,
affirming that the Uniates were actually Catholic, that their priests
were not in fact Orthodox. Just the year before, in 1773, Konys´kyi,
on the Orthodox side, had given the opposite interpretation,

---

112   Korczok, *Griechisch-katholische Kirche*, 29; see also Wolff, "Inventing
Galicia," 818–40.

113   Madey, *Kirche zwischen Ost und West*, 121.

insisting that the Uniates "preserved the Greek-Russian faith in their hearts and very often secretly went to Orthodox churches."[114] Catherine almost quoted him in 1782 when she wrote to the pope that the Uniates "await only the least signal to embrace our Orthodox religion, which they abandoned with regret, and of which they retain many traces and vestiges in their hearts." These exercises in identifying the Uniates, in designating them by their true names or in reading their hearts, were undertaken in these years by the Propaganda Fide and the St. Petersburg Synod, by Catherine and by Maria Theresa. Such interest from without, however, made it all the more urgent that the Uniate Church carry on its own self-analysis from within, and seek to define the terms of the Union compromise.

Early in the eighteenth century, at the Uniate Synod of Zamość in 1720, an ordering of the Uniate Church according to the concerns and ideals of Tridentine Catholicism initiated a significant Latinization of the rite. The most conspicuous reform was the introduction of the *filioque* into the credo, in opposition to the Orthodox theological doctrine that the Holy Spirit proceeds from the father alone. There followed in the 1730s a thorough revision of the liturgy, rendering it distinct from that of the Orthodox.[115] The construction of magnificent new Uniate cathedrals in the episcopal centers, St. George's in Lviv (finished in 1764) and St. Sophia's in Polatsk (finished in 1765), followed the architectural spirit of Roman Baroque, in marked contrast to the traditional Ruthenian wooden churches. St. George's, designed by Bernard Meretyn, actually attempted to unite Roman Catholic and Russian Orthodox architectural conceptions; the basic cruciform plan allowed for four slightly domed chapels around the great central dome, thus hinting at the five-domed Orthodox model. There was also an extravagantly Baroque Uniate church at Berazvechcha (Berezwecz, now part of Hlybokae, in Belarus),

---

114 Likowski, *Geschichte des allmaeligen Verfalls*, 1:190.
115 Madey, *Kirche zwischen Ost und West*, 78–80.

the church of the Basilians, where the facade was constructed of nine convex and eight concave surfaces.[116]

Resistance to Latinization within the Uniate Church found encouragement in the papal constitution of 1755, "Allatae sunt," with its assurance that Rome never intended "to cause any damage to the venerable Oriental rites" of the Uniates in Europe and the Middle East.[117] The linked Uniate concerns about Roman Catholic *praestantia*, Latin transit, and the Romanization of ritual acquired new urgency in the period that followed the partition of 1772. When Smohozhevs´kyi assured the ladies of St. Petersburg that "there exists no essential difference between my mass and those of Russia," the asserted identity had not been generally true for the last fifty years, since the Synod of Zamość. His commitment to that position, in the context of eighteenth-century controversy over the rite, was probably one reason why, after his stay in St. Petersburg, he found himself denounced in some quarters as a "most corrupt schismatic."[118]

In 1778 the Uniate bishops of Poland, in a memorial to the pope, not only called for the prohibition of transit, but also insisted that "the Greek rite be maintained most exactly, on account of its holiness, and also because of the temperament of the Greeks, most tenacious about their institutions."[119] The insistence on exact preservation in Poland matched Smohozhevs´kyi's commitment in Russia, and the explanatory reference to "tenacious temperament" very explicitly justified ritual practice by popular custom. The Uniate Church could not tolerate the Latinization of its rite because, with the decline of the Commonwealth, religious sur-

---

116 Zbigniew Dmochowski, *The Architecture of Poland: An Historical Survey* (London, 1956), 282–85; and Ammann, *Abriss der ostslawischen Kirchengeschichte*, 413–14; see also David Buxton, *The Wooden Churches of Eastern Europe* (Cambridge, 1981).

117 Korczok, *Griechisch-katholische Kirche*, 99.

118 Smogorzewski, *Epistolae*, 94.

119 *Acta S. C. de Propaganda Fide*, 5:100.

vival became all the more dependent upon meeting the spiritual needs and expectations of the social base. When Siestrzeńcewicz attempted to welcome Uniates into Roman Catholicism during the Polatsk vacancy of 1779–1783, he discovered that they could not accept the abrupt transition from the Greek to the Latin rite, and so he became himself the sponsor of a remarkable experiment in ritual. The Uniate clergy did not know enough Latin to celebrate a Latin mass, and so Siestrzeńcewicz ended up in the awkward position of allowing the Slavonic mass with just a few words of Latin, and calling it the Latin rite. Naturally, he had to allow the Uniate priests to keep their wives. The most important ritual concession that he demanded of his ex-Uniates as the sign of their transit was taking communion with unleavened bread. In short, he intended to eliminate the Greek rite of the Union and instead found himself creating a new union within the Latin rite, basically renegotiating the terms of the compromise. He even found himself publishing a special missal for the rite that he had invented.[120]

The Uniates could not be simply roped into the Latin rite, and the disorientation of the Uniate at a Roman Catholic mass was still worth noting two hundred years later when Andy Warhol, the American Pop artist of Carpathian-Ruthenian descent, attended mass in Manhattan in 1984. "I always cringe when it gets to the part of 'Peace, peace be with you,' and you have to shake hands with the people next to you," wrote Warhol in his diary. "I always leave before that. Or I pretend to be praying. I don't know how long they've done it because I went to the Greek Catholic church when I was young." Art criticism has noted the "Byzantine" quality in Warhol's famous silk-screen portraits of Marilyn Monroe and Elvis Presley.[121]

---

120 Likowski, *Geschichte des allmaeligen Verfalls*, 1:206.

121 Andy Warhol, *The Andy Warhol Diaries*, ed. Pat Hackett (New York, 1989), 580; Peter Schjeldahl, "Warhol in Bloom: Putting the Pop Artist in Perspective," *The New Yorker*, 11 March 2002, 84.

The great Uniate liturgical reform project of the 1780s was undertaken by Iraklii Lisovs´kyi, who finally filled the vacant archbishopric of Polatsk in 1783. His appointment, as the choice of Catherine and Potemkin, immediately cost the life of another Uniate bishop, Hedeon Horbats´kyi (Gedeon Horbacki), who had to rush across Belarus in the winter from Pinsk to Polatsk, to consecrate Lisovs´kyi before Catherine changed her mind about filling the vacancy; Horbats´kyi fell sick, and died soon after performing the consecration.[122] Lisovs´kyi became the most important Uniate in the Russian Empire through the next generation, the only Uniate bishop during the hard years from 1795 to 1798, and the new "Metropolitan of the Uniate Church in Russia" after 1806. During the vacancy in Polatsk from 1779 to 1783, one member of the three-man consistory, Malynovs´kyi, considered bringing the whole Uniate Church over to the Latin rite; Lisovs´kyi, who was also a member of that consistory, afterwards attempted as archbishop of Polatsk to bring the Uniates closer to the rituals of Orthodoxy. In 1787 the Propaganda Fide was presented with Lisovs´kyi's proposal for a comprehensive reform of Uniate ritual: "He believes it is necessary that all those ceremonies which destroy the antique Greek rite should be extirpated," thus eliminating the "censurable mix and affected imitation of Latin ceremonies" introduced after the synod of Zamość.[123] Just as Smohozhevs´kyi had challenged Rome in the 1770s to demonstrate the sincerity of the Union by prohibiting transit, now in the 1780s Lisovs´kyi demanded another demonstration of sincerity in the preservation of the rite.

Lisovs´kyi proposed revisions from the most invisible details of administering the sacraments to the most ostentatious ceremonies of public worship. He protested that Uniate sacraments and prayers had come to constitute a "corrupt mishmash" (*vizioso*

---

122 Likowski, *Geschichte des allmaeligen Verfalls*, 1:209.

123 *Acta S. C. de Propaganda Fide*, 5:148; see also Leonid Żytkowicz, "Lisowski, Józef (Heraclius)," *Polski Słownik Biograficzny*, vol. 17 (Cracow, 1972), 473-74.

miscuglio) of the Greek and Latin rites, but his arguments for reform were not based on purism and historicism alone. He wanted
to restore certain introits to the Uniate mass for the reason that
"this ceremony in the Oriental Church is quite antique, and very
magnificent, and also well adapted to excite devotion in the
heart of those present." His reform was intended to attract the
spiritual commitment of the Uniate population. Magnificence
alone, however, was not a sufficient criterion for revising the
rite, and he rejected organ music as a "ridiculous imitation of
the Latin rite," as "extraneous" to the Oriental liturgy and "the
custom of the nation."[124] Lisovs´kyi's attention to his position
within the Russian Empire was also evident in his concern lest
the Orthodox be "scandalized" by the Uniate "mishmash," and in
his proposal to reduce the number of Uniate holidays to satisfy
the economic interests of the Russian state. His reduction of the
religious festivals was certainly not random, since, in choosing
the most important days to be observed, he decided "according
to the custom of the Oriental Church." The Propaganda Fide was
troubled to see these did not include the feast of Saints Peter
and Paul on June 29—while allowing for a holiday on December
6, the feast of Saint Nicholas, patron of Russia.[125]

The Propaganda Fide in 1787 rejected Lisovs´kyi's reform,
ordering him "not to innovate at all, and especially not to permit
the use of the ritual that serves the non-Uniates."[126] The two
perspectives were poles apart, for Lisovs´kyi saw himself as the
enemy of innovations, and regarded the forbidden "ritual that
serves the non-Uniates" as none other than the Uniates' own
Greek rite. Rome denied Lisovs´kyi's affirmation that, according
to the terms of the Union compromise, the Uniate rite and the
Orthodox rite should be one and the same. In rejecting his reform,
the Roman Congregation did not hesitate to cast aspersions upon

---

124 *Acta S. C. de Propaganda Fide*, 5:150.

125 *Acta S. C. de Propaganda Fide*, 5:150–55.

126 *Acta S. C. de Propaganda Fide*, 5:155.

Lisovs´kyi's character and piety, especially for his sensitivity to the concerns of the Russian state and the "scandalized" Orthodox:

> It is quite extraordinary that a Catholic, an ecclesiastic, and much more a bishop, should bother himself about the criticism of the heterodox regarding rites that are in themselves not at all reprehensible, and even if they differ from antique custom have been authorized by subsequent use. This weakness will give courage to the non-Uniates to attack also the dogmas that do not please them, and it is to be feared that he who has not faced up to sustaining the less important observances, may feel that he lacks the courage to resist in matters of greater consequence.[127]

Lisovs´kyi, even more than Smohozhevs´kyi in the 1770s, found himself suspect in the eyes of Rome for his interpretation of the Union. He would prove very disappointing to Rome when it came to defending the Uniates against Catherine in the crisis of the 1790s, but the mistrust of the Propaganda Fide helped to fulfill its own prophecies. Whereas Rome obviously felt that Lisovs´kyi had demonstrated a deficient commitment to the Union in 1787, from his perspective he had every reason to attribute that deficiency to Rome.

When Lisovs´kyi's proposals were rejected, the Propaganda Fide suggested instead that he await the new missal that Smohozhevs´kyi had promised in 1780 when he assumed the metropolitanate. If Lisovs´kyi were to reform his own liturgy in Belarus, without reference to the Uniate Church in Poland, he would be causing undesirable "disorder." Smohozhevs´kyi was known to be "most committed" to publishing a revised missal, and had blocked the publication of any other Uniate missals until his own was ready, but unfortunately the work was not yet complete.[128] The abortive dialogue on liturgical reform between Lisovs´kyi

---

127 *Acta S. C. de Propaganda Fide*, 5:166.
128 *Acta S. C. de Propaganda Fide*, 5:167.

and the Propaganda Fide is strongly suggestive of the tensions and obstacles that Smohozhevs´kyi might have encountered in trying to produce his missal; little wonder that it was not yet ready after seven years. However, the fact that Lisovs´kyi in the Russian Empire and Smohozhevs´kyi in Poland were both working on revisions of ritual and liturgy in the 1780s was evidence of how important the issue had become for the Uniate Church.

While the missal remained unfinished, Smohozhevs´kyi did preside over the completion of the new Uniate Church of the Basilians on Ulica Miodowa in Warsaw in 1784—three years after the laying of the foundation stone in the presence of the Polish king. In its architectural style the new church illustrated the importance for the Uniates of defining their cultural and religious identity: designed by the Italian-Swiss architect Domenico Merlini, the moving spirit of Neoclassicism in the capital of Stanisław August and the creator of the king's marvelous palace and park at Łazienki, Smohozhevs´kyi boldly built his Warsaw church in the modern style of the decade, and put behind him the Counter-Reformation Baroque with all its troubling historical associations for the Uniates. "I have had built in Warsaw an elegant and spacious church," he wrote in 1783 to Pope Pius VI, himself a patron of Neoclassicism. This emphasis on "elegance" was almost ecumenical in its worldliness. Indeed, according to the architectural historian Zbigniew Dmochowski, from the outside "only an Eye of Providence surrounded by golden rays in the pediment indicated that the building was intended for religious purposes," while "the interior, similarly, was more in the character of a palace chamber than a church."[129] The Palladian facade, with its Neoclassical pointed pediment atop four stately pilasters, matched in spirit the historical evocation of Renaissance and

---

129   Dmochowski, *The Architecture of Poland*, 400; Julian Bartoszewicz, *Kościoły warszawskie* (Warsaw, 1855), 298–300; Jean Fabre, *Stanislas-Auguste Poniatowski et l'Europe des lumières* (Paris, 1952), 387–88.

Enlightenment by which Smohozhevs´kyi attempted to finesse the implications for the Union of the Jesuit Counter-Reformation.

Throughout this period, history played an important part in exploring and defining the Uniate identity. In 1775 Smohozhevs´kyi was collaborating with a Basilian monk in collecting documents for a history of the Uniates. In the upheavals surrounding the partition he had put the project aside "for lack of time and quiet," but he was no less committed to "putting before the eyes of the public the facts and the circumstances of the most antique Union of the Ruthenians." He reflected that "if this little work should see light in the present circumstances, it would illuminate the former and confirm the latter"—that is, illuminate the public and confirm the Uniates.[130] Smohozhevs´kyi thus sought to clarify the religious identity of the Uniates in the eighteenth century by documenting, interpreting, and publicizing the historical record of the Union; he was sufficiently modern in his approach to imagine the discourse of Uniate identity taking place in some sort of public sphere. In 1790, two years after Smohozhevs´kyi's death, the Propaganda Fide recommended to the Basilians that they carry on with the unfinished history project, and "the most intelligent and erudite monks" were assigned to collect documents for that purpose.[131] With the shaking of the ancien régime across Europe and the revolutionary reform of the Commonwealth in the Four-Year Sejm, it became all the more urgent for the Uniates, on the threshold of modern European history, to appreciate the early modern history of the Union.

Agitated by Scruples

In 1793, as the Uniates faced the daunting Orthodox campaign that accompanied the second and third partitions of Poland in the last years of Catherine's reign, there occurred an embarrass-

---

130   Smogorzewski, *Epistolae*, 175.
131   *Acta S. C. de Propaganda Fide*, 5:172.

ing incident within the Uniate episcopate. Ioakym Horbats´kyi (Joachim Horbacki), bishop of Pinsk, requested permission from the pope to abdicate his bishopric and adopt the Latin rite. Papal provision was required not only for the abdication but also for Horbats´kyi's "transit," an issue that had become highly sensitive over the previous half century. Horbats´kyi had, in fact, been originally ordained as a Roman Catholic priest, and then entered the Uniate Basilian order with the special understanding that he might preserve his Latin rite. As a Basilian monk he went on observing that Latin rite for twenty years, until "without his knowledge and without exploring his will," his superiors obtained permission from Rome to switch him to the Greek rite in 1777, in order to promote him to an abbacy and then to a bishopric. He became bishop of Pinsk in 1785, soon after the death of his brother Hedeon Horbats´kyi, the fatally unlucky traveler who braved the winter weather to consecrate Lisovs´kyi in Polatsk. After eight years as a Uniate bishop, Ioakym Horbats´kyi still claimed to have adopted the Greek rite "out of pure obedience and contrary to will," and admitted to great spiritual uneasiness about his "total ignorance" of the "Ruthenian language." This probably reflected a dual ignorance on the part of the Polish bishop, both of the Slavic vernacular appropriate to the pastoral care of his diocese and of the Church Slavonic necessary for his liturgical responsibilities. In Rome it was registered as something "monstrous" that a bishop should not know the language of his own rite.[132]

The investigation of this monstrosity led the Propaganda Fide to hear testimony from Bishop Vazhyns´kyi of Chełm, who as protoarchimandrite of the Basilians had arranged for Horbats´kyi's transit and promotion. Vazhyns´kyi had been Rome's candidate to fill the Polatsk vacancy in the early 1780s, until Catherine insisted on Lisovs´kyi; then Vazhyns´kyi in 1787 helped Rome find reasons to reject Lisovs´kyi's liturgical reforms. In 1794 Vazhyns´kyi would be the Uniate bishop most involved in the Kościuszko insurrection

---

132   *Acta S. C. de Propaganda Fide*, 5:187–88.

against Russia, while Lisovs´kyi was credited with an altogether too cautious, if not downright halfhearted, resistance to Catherine's campaign against the Uniates. Vazhyns´kyi thus represented both a Polish political and Latin liturgical interpretation of the Union, and, consistent with that perspective, he sponsored the promotion of the Latin-leaning Horbats´kyi to a top position in the Uniate hierarchy. When questioned by the Propaganda Fide in 1793, Vazhyns´kyi neither apologized for the promotion nor sympathized with the abdication. He testified thus:

> Now then, he complains that he doesn't know the Ruthenian
> language, and that he is agitated by scruples. I pity my confrere
> with all my soul, but if we consider well: who is that bishop who
> does not feel the weight of his bishopric and his weakness to bear
> it? And therefore I believe that the origin of his pusillanimity is
> his being a lover of solitude and a certain hypochondria generated
> by scruples.[133]

Vazhyns´kyi's confidence in the ecclesiastical ancien régime made his colleague's spiritual anxiety incomprehensible, except perhaps as psychological debility. In fact, Horbats´kyi's "scruples" were symptomatic inklings of a more modern religious consciousness.

Vazhyns´kyi did not see Horbats´kyi's linguistic incapacity as a meaningful motive for resigning, and neither was he shocked by the discovery of this crypto-Latin in the Uniate episcopate. "I know many in the Basilian order," he reported to Rome, "who were accepted coming from the Latin clergy, both secular and regular, and were then accustomed to retain perseveringly until death their Latin rite." This frank admission was occasioned by the following awkwardly defensive note by the Propaganda Fide: "The custom of receiving into the Ruthenian Basilian order many of the Latin clergy, both regular and secular, who further retain constantly within that order their Latin rite, cannot be

---

133 *Acta S. C. de Propaganda Fide*, 5:190.

said to be properly approved by the Holy See."[134] The Propaganda Fide thus had to acknowledge that the Basilian order was a
bastion of Roman Catholic influence within the Uniate Church,
and this rendered the Horbats´kyi case as awkward in Rome as
in Pinsk; it cast doubt upon Vatican assurances of Uniate ritual
independence just as Catherine was inaugurating her campaign
against the Uniates. In fact, while Rome was concerned about
the "scandal" of a Uniate bishop who knew nothing of the Greek
rite, Vazhyns´kyi thought even greater scandal would come from
allowing Horbats´kyi the desired transit to return to Roman Catholicism. He recommended that Horbats´kyi be retired to the
privacy of a Basilian monastery, and not be allowed transit unless
he decided to resettle in Rome—"where he could pick up again the
Latin rite without scandal." In the final decree, he was permitted
to celebrate the Latin mass, but only "in Oratorio privato."[135] The
story of Horbats´kyi would have had some propaganda value in
the Orthodox campaign then under way, so the whole affair was
disposed of as discreetly as possible. It was Catherine who really
spared Rome the embarrassment of negotiating an episcopal
succession—by abolishing the Pinsk diocese in 1795.

The promotion and abdication of Horbats´kyi clearly suggests the critical issues of clergy and culture in the internal
development of the Uniate Church at the end of the eighteenth
century. The competing influences of the Latin and Greek rites
were reflected in the internal organization of the Church itself, in
the separation and alienation of the privileged Basilian order, with
its crypto-Latin elements, from the ritual values of the secular
clergy and peasant laity. The compromise that created the Uniate
Church—between Roman authority and Greek ritual—was both
supplemented and subtly undermined by the de facto internal
compromise between monastic privilege and peasant society. After
1772, attention to the terms of the greater compromise, from with-

---

134   *Acta S. C. de Propaganda Fide*, 5:188.
135   *Acta S. C. de Propaganda Fide*, 5:190–91.

out and from within, put revolutionary pressures upon the lesser compromise, and ultimately reordered the balance of power and privilege within the Uniate Church. The "scruples" of Horbats´kyi in 1793 reflected those pressures, for it was becoming harder and harder to ignore the disparities between ecclesiastical privilege and popular piety in an age of revolution. His self-reproach on account of "ignorance" was particularly interesting, inasmuch as it echoed a common preoccupation of the time, at all levels of the Uniate Church, combining the concerns of Counter-Reformation and Enlightenment. Horbats´kyi's self-proclaimed ignorance was at once linguistic and ritual, and though he was an educated churchman, not at all ignorant in the popular sense of the word, his particular ignorance disqualified him in his own opinion from being a Uniate. Nothing could indicate more clearly that there was indeed emerging at this time a distinct conception of Uniate identity, one that would challenge both clergy and laity to accept or deny their affiliation according to a new religious standard.

At the Synod of Zamość in 1720, at the same time that a degree of liturgical Latinization was introduced into the Uniate Church, the Basilian monks consolidated formally their remarkable ecclesiastical power. The crucial point was the synod's decision that Uniate bishops had to come from the Basilian order, and the justification was that bishops had to be celibate. Within the Uniate Church the secular parish clergy were permitted to marry, like the Orthodox clergy, while the Basilian regular clergy took a vow of chastity. Any secular priest who aspired to the episcopate would first have to seek entry into the Basilian order, and then wait within the order for one year and six weeks. Convening at Dubno in 1743, the Basilians further magnified the power assigned to them at Zamość by organizing themselves under the authority of a single protoarchimandrite, and asserting in that organization their independence from the bishops—who were anyway chosen from the Basilian ranks. Such power manifested itself in the Basilian appropriation of the richest benefices in the Uniate Church, and the most prestigious educational opportunities, especially in

Rome. There were more than a thousand Basilian monks in the Commonwealth in the eighteenth century, possessing wealth, influence, and learning that dramatically contrasted with the condition of the parish clergy. John-Paul Himka has remarked that "while the Basilians flourished, the Ukrainian secular clergy languished."[136]

The Vatican inevitably felt ambivalent about the Basilian monopoly of power and privilege among the Uniates. As demonstrated in the case of Ioakym Horbats´kyi in 1793, the Basilians represented a distinctly Latin force within the Uniate Church, and it was no mere coincidence that their consolidation of power at Zamość should have coincided with the commencement of eighteenth-century Latinization. While the Uniates deplored the transit of the laity to Roman Catholicism, ambitious Roman Catholic priests were entering Uniate monasteries, which offered excellent chances for ecclesiastical advancement. Vazhyns´kyi claimed to know "many" Basilians of Roman Catholic origin, while one estimate suggested that they constituted almost half the monks. Their monopoly on higher theological training—not only at the Greek College in Rome, but even in Jesuit and Piarist institutions—meant that they also were the only Uniates who wrote about theology, naturally with sympathy for the Latin perspective. It was Vazhyns´kyi as protoarchimandrite who counseled the Propaganda Fide to reject Lisovs´kyi's reform of Latin liturgical intrusions in 1787, and the Basilian order gathered in 1788 to express its collective rejection of Lisovs´kyi. This Latin bias did not, however, make the Basilians any more militantly resistant to Russian Orthodox pressures during this period. Instead, their vested economic interests favored a cautious conciliation of Catherine.[137]

---

136 John-Paul Himka, "The Conflict between the Secular and the Religious Clergy in Eighteenth-Century Western Ukraine," *Harvard Ukrainian Studies* 15, no. 1-2 (June 1991): 37-39; Likowski, *Geschichte des allmaeligen Verfalls*, 1:292.

137 Likowski, *Geschichte des allmaeligen Verfalls*, 1:293; Korczok, *Griechisch-*

In the first half of the eighteenth century the Basilians rose
to the peak of their power and influence, but in the second half
they found themselves seriously embattled and ultimately van-
quished. In 1747 the secular clergy in the dioceses of Lviv and
Przemyśl submitted a memorial to Pope Benedict XIV protesting
against the monks' appropriation of all the richest benefices
for themselves. In 1749 Lev Sheptyts´kyi became archbishop of
Lviv, and, though himself a Basilian, he refused to accept that his
appointment required the permission of the protoarchimandrite;
Sheptyts´kyi even excluded the monks from the procession that
celebrated his episcopal installation. Furthermore, he proceeded
to engage in a long conflict of property with the Basilians for
possession of rich estates and important churches, including the
cathedral of St. George in Lviv itself.[138] The coincident timing of
the Latin assertion of precedence in "Etsi pastoralis" (1742) and
the Basilian self-assertion at Dubno (1743) made possible a dual
resistance: to Latin predominance from outside and to Basilian
predominance within the Uniate Church. These concerns fed upon
each other quite plausibly, inasmuch as many Basilians were in
fact Latin-leaning Uniates.

In 1771 Sheptyts´kyi inaugurated the campaign that would
continue through the decade and for the rest of his life, to break
the power of the Basilians by creating a cathedral chapter of
secular priests in Lviv to assist in the administration of the diocese. His intention was to establish an institution that would give
ecclesiastical power to the secular clergy and end the Basilian
monopoly. It was most revealing that the champion of the Uniate
monks was none other than the Roman Catholic archbishop of
Lviv, Sierakowski, the same who represented the causes of transit
to the Latin rite and Roman Catholic episcopal predominance.

---

katholische Kirche, 16–18; Ammann, Abriss der ostslawischen Kirchengeschichte, 437.

138 Ammann, Abriss der ostslawischen Kirchengeschichte, 420–21; Himka,
"Conflict between the Secular and the Religious Clergy," 40–41.

By entering the lists against Sheptyts´kyi, Sierakowski matched himself against his Uniate counterpart in Lviv and posed the question of predominance in the form of personal combat. The partition of Poland in 1772 assigned Lviv to Austria, and so Sheptyts´kyi's challenge to the monks was carried on under the more favorable auspices of Maria Theresa. The breaking of Basilian power in this period was unmistakably related to the collapse of the Commonwealth and the emergence of new political circumstances. For Maria Theresa the principle of equal rites meant that the Uniate bishops were just as entitled to cathedral chapters as the Latin bishops. In 1774 she issued a statement to that effect: "Regarding the erection of a Greek-Uniate chapter in Lemberg [Lviv], the reception of the Union cannot be more excellent than when one observes between the Uniate and the Latin rites a perfect equality in externals, and on the other hand seeks to put aside all that could make the Uniate people believe they are thought worse than the Roman Catholics."[139] State confirmation of the Lviv chapter was frustrated, however, by the deaths of Sheptyts´kyi in 1779 and Maria Theresa herself in 1780. Joseph created not chapters but consistories of lay officials who were marked as the emperor's men, not the bishop's, by their inscribed pectoral crosses. Resistance to the Habsburg establishment of the metropolitanate itself in 1806 was conducted by an alliance of Basilians and Roman Catholic clergy.

By that time the Basilians were in serious decline, for the campaign of Sheptyts´kyi in the 1770s, though it fell short of actually obtaining the chapter, was nevertheless effective in rallying Uniate forces and sentiments against the monks. In the year of his death, 1779, he decisively won his property dispute with the monks over control of St. George's in Lviv; in that same

---

139 Korczok, *Griechisch-katholische Kirche*, 58–61; Himka, "Conflict between the Secular and the Religious Clergy," 42–44; see also Iryna Vushko, *The Politics of Cultural Retreat: Imperial Bureaucracy in Austrian Galicia, 1772–1867* (New Haven: Yale University Press, 2015), 167–69.

year the Propaganda Fide in Rome censured Basilian presumption, and Maria Theresa affirmed her right to nominate a bishop who was not a Basilian. This she promptly proceeded to do when Sheptyts´kyi died, for, in spite of the stipulation of the Synod of Zamość, Maria Theresa chose as his successor a man of the secular clergy, Petro Bilians´kyi, thus shattering the Basilian grip on the Uniate episcopate. Furthermore, the empress, in the last year of her life, refused to allow even a token concession to the violated Basilian privilege, and forbade Bilians´kyi to seek any special dispensation from the Vatican for his appointment. Giuseppe Garampi, transferred to the Vienna nunciature from Warsaw, conspired in vain with Maria Theresa's confessor to alter her resolution. In thus affirming the sovereignty of her own selection, the empress attacked the keystone of Basilian power in the Uniate Church. Sheptyts´kyi was not the only Uniate bishop to rise from the Basilian ranks and turn against his former brothers; Smohozhevs´kyi, as metropolitan in Poland, consummated the ecclesiastical revolution by giving episcopal consecration to Bilians´kyi.[140]

In 1780 the Basilians convened to try to adapt themselves administratively to the post-partition political order. They were divided into four "provinces"—Poland, Lithuania, Austrian Poland, and Russian Poland—all theoretically under one protoarchimandrite, Vazhyns´kyi. The illusion of adaptation, however, was shattered in 1782 when Joseph II ruled out any subordination of the Basilians of Galicia to the protoarchimandrite in Poland; instead he placed them under the authority of the bishops. With Catherine's encouragement Lisovs´kyi sought the same subordination of the Basilians of Russian Poland, and they opposed his liturgical reforms with all the more fervor. When the order convened in 1790, the monks complained to Rome of Lisovs´kyi's "despotism." They pleaded desperately with "the greatest urgency" that the

---

140 Korczok, *Griechisch-katholische Kirche*, 54–55; Himka, "Conflict between the Secular and the Religious Clergy," 44–46.

Propaganda Fide "apply some brake to the excessive dominion that Monsignor Lisovs´kyi, archbishop of Polatsk, exercises over the monks and monasteries of that part of the kingdom of Poland now subject to the empress of Russia." The monks hoped that Rome would "wish to deign to put some dam to the imminent destruction of monasticism."[141] Whether the metaphor was brakes or dams, it clearly suggested the ongoing, irreversible drive or flow of power and privilege away from the Basilians in the second half of the eighteenth century. The struggle itself endowed the bishops and the secular clergy with new levels of energy and commitment to the Union. After such assaults the Basilian order was particularly vulnerable to the confiscations and appropriations carried out by Joseph in the 1780s and by Catherine in the 1790s, but the crucial challenge had already been posed from within the Uniate Church.

Asini

In September 1772, just as the partition was consummated, Smohozhevs´kyi in Polatsk requested from the Warsaw nunciature emergency ecclesiastical reinforcements in the moment of crisis, as Catherine became the sovereign of Belarus:

> It is supremely necessary that Monsignor nuncio should recommend immediately to the general of the Basilians that he send here as fast as he can to my cathedral erudite and prudent monks, obliged to counsel and aid the faithful…so that without resistance, at my disposition and according to my orders, they may visit the parishes, correct the defects that they find there, sustain and confirm the weak in faith, reduce to obedience the suspect, and constrain even rebels with the force of command. Without that how could one avert evil? Behold the effects of the Union depressed. What fruit is to be had from the independent Basilians? There

---

141   *Acta S. C. de Propaganda Fide,* 5:178.

are thirty of them here, and I can't make use of any of them. The
prior is distracted by governing the convent, the lecturers by their
obligation to teach, the others go to choir, and those that remain
are just young students. So what do they serve for? It's impossible
to make use of the secular priests, because they are occupied with
the care of their parishes, and their families, and for the most part
they are extremely ignorant (*ignorantissimi*).[142]

Here in 1772 Smohozhevs´kyi drew clearly the contrast between
the *eruditi* and the *ignorantissimi*—that is, between Basilian monks
and parish priests. At the same time, he posed the problem of
episcopal authority, summoning the monks "at my disposition
and according to my orders." He even frankly invoked a standard
of utility concerning the monks, asking "what fruit is to be had"
of them, how to "make use of any of them," and "what do they
serve for?"

Such expressions called into question the whole raison d'être
of the order, and were evidently provoked by the shock of the
partition crisis with its menacing political implications for the
Uniate Church. Smohozhevs´kyi's language was peculiarly close
to that of the anticlerical Enlightenment with its mockery of the
monastic orders. The next year in Warsaw there was published
anonymously an enlightened denunciation of monasticism in
general, with a similar refrain: "Why nourish in the stable an an-
imal that does nothing?"[143] In 1773 the suppression of the Jesuits
also presented an alarming precedent to all the orders of Europe.

Right after Smohozhevs´kyi contrasted Basilian erudition
with parish clerical ignorance in September 1772, he went on
to make the same pointed comparison in October with an interesting variation of terms. "For the love of the Jesuits it is not
fitting to keep in ignorance the secular clergy of the Uniates," he
wrote, "and now what use can I have from my poor and ignorant

142 Smogorzewski, *Epistolae*, 64.

143 Wolff, *The Vatican and Poland*, 87.

priests?"[144] In this case the ignorance and poverty of the parish clergy was emphasized by comparison to the privileged Jesuits, rather than the Basilians, and, considering Smohozhevs´kyi's hatred of the former, one may infer his considerable ambivalence toward the latter. The casting of the Jesuits and Basilians in this same role revealed a Uniate perspective in which Latin forces appeared to monopolize the precious resources of wealth and education without making them available to the urgent work of Uniate adaptation and survival in an age of crisis. The intellectual disparity between regular and secular clergy was addressed as a problem already at Zamość in 1720, and the synod mandated that monasteries should provide theological schooling for local secular priests. The monks, however, did not embrace this mission, and Basilian schools tended to serve the privileged laity; they could even be compared to Jesuit colleges.[145] In fact, after the suppression of the Jesuits in 1773 the Basilians were able to take over some of those colleges and run them successfully.

In 1774, half a century after Zamość prescribed the remedy, Smohozhevs´kyi was expressing his dissatisfaction to the Warsaw nuncio:

> I am now uniquely tormented by uncertainty about the true love and sincere commitment of the monks, not well disposed to the secular clergy for the good education of its youth; because to despise, to mistreat, and to educate fraudulently would be the same as to cool in the clergy the will to study, and to encourage ignorance for the extermination of the Catholic religion. Therefore, to avoid such enormities and dangers, it would be most convenient if Your Excellency would recommend to the monastic order better

---

144 Smogorzewski, *Epistolae*, 69.

145 Likowski, *Geschichte des allmaeligen Verfalls*, 1:289; M.M. Wojnar, "Ukrainian (Ruthenian) Rite," *New Catholic Encyclopedia*, vol. 14 (New York, 1967), 373.

affection for the secular clergy and the highest commitment to
their most efficacious education.[146]

At the same time that Maria Theresa was calling upon the Roman
Catholics of Galicia to "love" the Uniates, in Belarus it was nec-
essary to solicit the "affection" of the Basilians for their fellow
Uniate priests.

In the 1770s, the struggle over the Lviv chapter was already
under way, and the Basilians had good reason to feel embattled.
Smohozhevs´kyi's distrust of their "sincerity," his suspicion of
a "fraudulent" education intended to "cool" intellectual aspi-
rations, suggests an awareness of social struggle in which the
Basilians could not wholeheartedly teach theology to the parish
clergy without compromising their vested interests of power and
wealth. It was the Uniate episcopate, seeking to make "use" and
have "fruit" of its clergy that had to insist upon the "dangers"
of clerical ignorance and seek its remedy in "efficacious education." Ignorance and education became the great rallying cries
of the Uniate Church in the troubled age of the partitions, and
in the meanings that attached to those concepts one may trace
the values and strategies that guided the evolution of a modern
religious consciousness in the Uniate clergy.

Iosyf Shumlians´kyi (Józef Szumlański), the bishop of Lviv
who brought his diocese with him from Orthodoxy to the Union
in 1700, addressed the shortcomings of his clergy in very different
terms. "The priest," he instructed, "should always, and especially
when he goes to church for divine service, wear clean clothes,
not dirty, have his hair and beard combed, his hands washed,
his nails clipped."[147] Such a lesson, far from stressing religious
standards in the spirit of the Counter-Reformation, emphasized
the social chasm between the clerical elite and the parish clergy.
This chasm was not just a matter of neat nails and clean clothes,
for Uniate secular priests were, socioeconomically speaking,

---

146 Smogorzewski, *Epistolae*, 141.

147 Korczok, *Griechisch-katholische Kirche*, 13.

close to the peasants. The parish income came from a plot of land assigned to the priest and usually farmed by him with his own hands. Such farm work was spared the elite Basilian monks, with their teaching responsibilities and choir attendance, though Basilian nuns sometimes had to work as servant maids.[148] The parish priest was not even an absolutely free peasant, since he could sometimes be drafted for compulsory feudal labor. The persistence of this element of villeinage was demonstrated by the fact that it had to be formally forbidden in Galicia by Maria Theresa in 1777. In Poland there was even a feudal regression in clerical status in 1764, when the Sejm inaugurated the reign of Stanisław August by making the sons of Uniate priests subject to enserfment if they did not learn a trade or follow their fathers into the clergy. This, too, had to be legally repealed at the Four-Year Sejm in 1792: "When a priest of this rite comes from the peasant order, and after being liberated by his lord receives ordination, so in consequence of this passage into the ecclesiastical order not only he, but also his descendants of both sexes, will be regarded as free."[149]

It was sometimes difficult for Roman Catholics to take quite seriously the priestly status of men with wives and children, "descendants of both sexes." In fact, the Uniate clergy became a virtually hereditary caste in the seventeenth and eighteenth centuries, with sons of priests constituting as much as 85 percent of the clergy in some regions. On the one hand, this created a social separation from the enserfed peasantry, but, on the other hand, the hereditary expectation of a benefice encouraged resignation to ignorance, since there was only limited motivation for study. A Uniate commission of 1765 stressed the importance of encouraging priests to undertake the religious education of

148   Madey, *Kirche zwischen Ost und West*, 115.
149   Likowski, *Geschichte des allmaeligen Verfalls*, 1:303.

their own children, starting at the age of five, since those children were probably the priests of the next generation.[150]

By the middle of the eighteenth century there was already a clearly perceived conjunction of ecclesiastical ignorance and socioeconomic status. In 1747 the secular clergy protested the Basilian appropriation of the best benefices, and in 1748 Floriian Hrebnyts´kyi (Florian Hrebnicki) assumed the metropolitanate and evaluated clerical conditions. He feared that Uniate priests could not "in good conscience" be proposed for benefices, "because the candidates for the ecclesiastical order are in general so *rudes*."[151] The Latin term embraced a range of qualities, from wild and ignorant to uncultured and uncivilized. Indeed, taken together with Shumlians´kyi's attention to personal habits, Hrebnyts´kyi's verdict suggests that this eighteenth-century discourse on the Uniate clergy was partly stimulated by the forces of what Norbert Elias has called "the civilizing process," which involved increasing cultural attention to issues of manners between the sixteenth and the eighteenth centuries.[152]

Yet the ordination of priests in significant number, however ignorant, was absolutely essential to the pastoral care of the Uniate populations. Ludomir Bieńkowski has estimated that in 1772 there were 10,200 parish priests for 9,340 parishes, generally one priest to a parish, with each serving, on average, 800 to 1,000 people.[153] Considering the questionable quality of the candidates, Hrebnyts´kyi thought he might never ordain anyone "if it weren't a matter of letting the people die without baptism and sacraments." He also appreciated the crucial connection between economic and intellectual factors: "Whoever has a higher education doesn't

---

150 Ludomir Bieńkowski, "Organizacja Kościoła Wschodniego," 963–68; Senyk, "The Education of the Secular Clergy," 412.

151 Likowski, *Geschichte des allmaeligen Verfalls*, 1:285.

152 See Norbert Elias, *The History of Manners*, trans. Edmund Jephcott, The Civilizing Process, vol. 1 (New York, 1978).

153 Bieńkowski, "Organizacja Kościoła Wschodniego," 957–58.

choose this order, where the benefices are so poor, but looks around for something more lucrative." In 1782 Smohozhevs´kyi made the same connection, explaining the impossibility of finding educated candidates to embrace a life of peasant labors, "persecuted by the Catholic masters and furthermore plagued by the Jews."[154] He might have added that the Uniate bishops themselves played a role in the economic oppression of their own parish clergy. They claimed a yearly contribution from the priests of the diocese, and in some cases collected it with extortionate violence. The metropolitan Volodkovych, whose fitness for the episcopate was challenged in the 1760s and 1770s, asserted his dominion over the diocese by collecting from his clergy with the accompaniment of an armed guard. The bishop of Lutsk, Kypriian Stets´kyi (Cyprian Stecki), was apparently even more shameless, and around 1780 his clergy complained to Rome that he was enriching himself by a combination of simony, extortion, and confiscation, having the priests beaten and imprisoned when they resisted the impositions of his "pastoral visitations."[155] Some of his clerical victims apostatized to Orthodoxy, and in fact his methods of episcopal administration were not so dissimilar from the persecutions practiced by Russian troops and Orthodox proselytizers at the time of the first and the last partitions. These instances of episcopal oppression were only the most flagrant manifestations of the social and cultural polarization of privilege in the Uniate Church.

The eighteenth-century memoirs of Adam Moszczyński explicitly rated the Uniate parish clergy as more ignorant than its Roman Catholic counterpart, and noted that the Uniate priests "could scarcely read the psalter and the missal, knew neither moral theology nor religious doctrine, and were full of superstitions and prejudices."[156] From his perspective as a non-Uniate layman,

---

154   Likowski, *Geschichte des allmaeligen Verfalls*, 1:181, 285.

155   Likowski, *Geschichte des allmaeligen Verfalls*, 1:242, 302.

156   Likowski, *Geschichte des allmaeligen Verfalls*, 1:285.

Moszczyński was, ironically, better able to put his finger on the precisely religious significance of clerical ignorance. The failings that he enumerated were far from unprecedented in the history of Catholicism, since, according to Jean Delumeau, writing on the Counter-Reformation, the Roman Catholic Church had addressed itself to the same problem in the seventeenth century. St. Vincent de Paul, who died in 1660 and was canonized in 1737, devoted missionary work to remedying clerical ignorance in the French countryside, and discovered priests who did not even know the words of absolution.[157] With standards somewhat improved in Catholic Western Europe in the eighteenth century, it would become conventional for enlightened Western travelers to comment disapprovingly on the religious ignorance of the clergy and laity in Orthodox Eastern Europe.[158]

Smohozhevs´kyi, in his most quotable comment on the Uniate parish clergy, declared, "I cannot entrust them with the more important posts because they are *asini*."[159] With casual vulgarity he called them asses, and the word *asini,* taken together with *rudes* from Hrebnyts´kyi, again revealed the broad assumption of social distance between the clerical elite and the parish clergy. There was even perhaps some significance in the fact that these two grandees of the Greek rite should have chosen to express their condescension in Latin, a language of which their Uniate clerical inferiors were quite excusably ignorant. Smohozhevs´kyi, upon his return from St. Petersburg in 1773, requested a Basilian monk as his coadjutor assistant, and the job description showed that his time at Catherine's court had given the archbishop a high standard of ecclesiastical courtliness:

---

157   Delumeau, *Catholicism between Luther and Voltaire,* 159.

158   Larry Wolff, *The Enlightenment and the Orthodox World: Western Perspectives on the Orthodox Church in Eastern Europe* (Athens: Institute for Neohellenic Research, 2001).

159   Likowski, *Geschichte des allmaeligen Verfalls,* 1:193.

It would be convenient therefore, and necessity requires, that
I should be provided without delay with a monk, well known,
capable of the courtesy of the century (*della polizia del secolo*), not
awkward, not bigoted, well educated, versed in theology, accustomed to working at a desk, of manly age, of upright habits, of
amiable conversation...[160]

It was naturally unnecessary to mention that such a paragon
would have neatly combed hair and evenly clipped fingernails.
This ideal ecclesiastic appeared to be some sort of descendant
of Baldassare Castiglione's Renaissance courtier; here again the
history of the Uniates intersected with the history of manners.

With this ideal in mind, however, Smohozhevsʹkyi went right
on in the same dispatch to address the issue of the uncourtly
parish clergy and the importance of elevating its standard. He
began with the paradox of the size of his diocese, geographically
"most vast," and yet effectively so small, "because it lacks good
workers," effective parish priests:

While with Jesuitical zeal it was despoiled of its own fattest
benefices, and without seminaries, it was served by priests hardly
adequate, indeed altogether ignorant. Since the first hours of my
pastorate, sympathizing with the unhappy situation of this clergy
and this Church, I began in the name of God to put aside something
every year.[161]

He was saving to build a seminary to metamorphose the *asini*.
The urgency of this intention was measured by the conjunction
of "the universal ignorance of the clergy" and the "dangerous
neighborhood," that is, the Russian Empire. To make up for past
Jesuitical despoliation, he sought possession of confiscated Jesuit
property for Uniate educational purposes in 1774, and formulat-

---

160   Smogorzewski, *Epistolae*, 96.
161   Smogorzewski, *Epistolae*, 97.

ed his need in terms of competition with the Orthodox clergy. "I seek nothing for myself," he began, seeming to fear that some might not believe in his concern for the secular clergy. "I desire only justice, and try to educate better my clergy, for when even the schismatic priests are beginning to study, why must mine rot (*marcire*) in their antique ignorance?"[162] In short, it was the partition, assigning his diocese to the Russian Empire, that made his sympathy into purposeful policy.

He petitioned for educational opportunities in Rome and at the Pontifical College in Vilnius, so that the Uniate priests might "advantageously toil in the vineyard of Christ, here uncultivated (*incolta*) and very much in jeopardy (*periclitante*)."[163] The allegorical reference to toiling in the vineyard was perhaps tactless, considering that these priests did literally labor in the fields, but the concept of "cultivation" emphasized the problem of ignorance. The word *incolta* could signify both an "uncultivated" vineyard and an "uneducated" or "uncultured" soul, and it was that lack of cultivation, in parish priests and in their parishioners, which put the whole Uniate Church at risk in the age of the partitions. Smohozhevs´kyi was in Belarus, but he recognized the significance of Orthodox pressure and Uniate apostasy in Ukraine. Indeed, even Belarus was not altogether tranquil: "Frightened by the new government, several parish priests abandoned their churches and broke their vows, while others, being provoked, threatened, and even persecuted by the contrary clergy, began to vacillate in the Holy Union."[164] The idea of "vacillation" conveyed even more clearly the danger of clerical ignorance in the Uniate Church. For the Union, which had been created in compromise between Orthodoxy and Catholicism, was now menaced from both sides by pressures to apostasy and to transit; it could not survive in a condition of ongoing vacillation.

---

162 Smogorzewski, *Epistolae*, 97, 115.

163 Smogorzewski, *Epistolae*, 97.

164 Smogorzewski, *Epistolae*, 98.

Clerical education thus came to signify something quite specific: not just the general cultivation of the mind, but the inculcation of a Uniate identity. In this sense Horbats′kyi, a member of the educated episcopal elite, could characterize himself as "ignorant" for knowing only the Latin rite. Just as the seventeenth-century Counter-Reformation involved teaching the Catholics of Europe to reject Protestantism, so eighteenth-century Uniates, clergy and laity, ceased to be ignorant when they had learned that they were neither Roman Catholic nor Orthodox.

A crucial obstacle to educating the secular clergy was the very limited number of places open for advanced religious study. There were four places for the Uniates in the Greek College of St. Athanasius in Rome, and at the beginning of the eighteenth century the Synod of Zamość arranged for another ten places at the Theatine College in Lviv that educated both Ruthenians and Armenians. A total of 192 Ruthenian Uniates studied at the Lviv school in the eighteenth century, though some ultimately became Basilian monks rather than parish priests. Because of the limited educational opportunities there were Uniate priests who actually ended up studying in Orthodox schools in Kyiv and Pereiaslav, or even in Moldova and Wallachia—and this was hardly likely to nourish a commitment to the Union. The Vilnius Pontifical College had been established in 1582, before the Union, for the missionary purpose of educating Russians and Ruthenians, but instead it was Roman Catholic students who largely filled its rosters; only in the eighteenth century was there a concerted Uniate effort to claim the seminary for themselves, beginning with a memorandum to Rome in 1753. Smohozhevs′kyi, who appreciated the perils of clerical ignorance, was still dickering in 1774 for places at the Vilnius seminary: "So I will not fail to choose two capable youths to send to Rome next autumn, and I will have ready others for whenever there occurs some vacancy in the College of Vilnius."[165] Smohozhevs′kyi might have worried

---

165   Smogorzewski, *Epistolae*, 139; Bieńkowski, "Organizacja Kościoła

about the Jesuit tradition at the Vilnius seminary, but in 1774 the society was already formally suppressed.

Above all, the Uniate Church lacked those Tridentine diocesan seminaries sponsored by the Counter-Reformation for the Roman Catholic clergy all over Europe. In 1759 Maksymiliian Ryllo managed to open a seminary for his diocese of Chełm. In 1763 Syl´vester Rudnyts´kyi (Sylvester Rudnicki), bishop of Lutsk, established a seminary there, but after his death in 1777 and a major fire in 1779, the funds were appropriated by his successor, Kypriian Stets´kyi, who was actually hostile to clerical education. In 1773 Smohozhevs´kyi was saving money to build a seminary of his own at Polatsk. In 1774 he had prepared plans for its construction, and submitted them to the Russian government. In 1775 he had still not heard from the government, blamed the ill will of the Orthodox Synod, and suspended his preparations for building, resolving to build across the border in Poland if he couldn't in the Russian Empire.[166] In 1776 a seminary opened in Zhytomyr for Ukraine, after the Orthodox pressures had ebbed, and in the 1780s Smohozhevs´kyi worked toward the establishment of a seminary at his metropolitan residence in Radomyshl. In 1774 Maria Theresa gave her Uniates the Barbaraeum in Vienna with fourteen places, but the most spectacular breakthrough in Uniate clerical education came in 1782 in Galicia with Joseph's program of state seminaries. Thus, the Counter-Reformation came to the Uniate Church belatedly, in the late eighteenth century, under the sponsorship of enlightened absolutism. The Lviv Theatine College and the Barbaraeum were eliminated in favor of the Josephine General Seminary in Lviv, which opened in 1783 with fifty-two places, and in 1787 that was supplemented by the Ruthenian Institute.[167]

Wschodniego," 974–75; Senyk, "Education of the Secular Clergy," 407–8.

166   Smogorzewski, *Epistolae*, 148, 175; Bieńkowski, "Organizacja Kościoła Wschodniego," 977–80.

167   Korczok, *Griechisch-katholische Kirche*, 46–48; Bieńkowski, "Organizacja

In Poland the Four-Year Sejm legislated the founding of Uniate diocesan seminaries in 1790, but the final partitions made these no more than good intentions. The enlightened Polish patriot Hugo Kołłątaj observed the educational developments of the Uniate Church with interest, noting that the clergy was still insufficiently "enlightened." He wrote in particular about the seminary at Lutsk established by Rudnytsʹkyi ("an enlightened man," in Kołłątaj's judgment) and regretted that there was too much theology taught and too little of other subjects. Yet even comprehensive instruction in theology was an advance for the Uniate clergy, and the commitment to educational improvement was notable enough so that Kołłątaj could evaluate the Uniates according to the contemporary standard of enlightenment. Sophia Senyk, writing about Ruthenian religion in historical perspective, has noted that "the formation of the secular clergy did not vary greatly from the time of the introduction of Christianity in Rusʹ in the tenth century until the end of the eighteenth." Change did come about, however, in the eighteenth century. In the historical judgment of Bieńkowski, "the matter of proper education for the parish clergy was not fully resolved at the conclusion of the existence of the Commonwealth, but progress achieved in this field in the course of the second half of the eighteenth century was indubitably significant."[168]

Short of formal seminary education, Uniate bishops in this period were attempting to achieve a higher standard of religious awareness among their parish priests by imposing examinations. It was in this context of stricter regulation that Vazhynsʹkyi, bishop of Chełm after 1790, achieved a certain notoriety for his low standard in ordaining priests. Hrebnytsʹkyi and Smohozhevsʹkyi both felt obliged to explain the ignorance of the clergy by reference to the poverty of the posts, but Vazhynsʹkyi was said to be

Kościoła Wschodniego," 980–81.

168 Bieńkowski, "Organizacja Kościoła Wschodniego," 978–81; Senyk, "Education of the Secular Clergy," 389.

untroubled in his easy ordinations. He expected the candidates
to know a little ritual, and to pay a fee, but when challenged by
another bishop regarding their general ignorance, Vazhyns'kyi is
supposed to have airily replied, "Omnis spiritus laudet dominum"
(Let every spirit praise the Lord).[169] Sheptyts'kyi, whose commitment to the secular clergy was expressed in his campaign for the
cathedral chapter at Lviv, established in his diocese a system of
examinations that set a new standard, and made Vazhyns'kyi's
amenability seem irresponsible by comparison. Sheptyts'kyi
insisted that his priests be examined quarterly, and that the
demonstration of theological competency be the condition of
receiving a benefice.[170]

Sheptyts'kyi also was interested in decorations to reward
those who met new standards of piety, and in 1770 obtained the
permission of Pope Clement XIV to bestow an honorary cross on
a gold chain.[171] Joseph II had all the cathedral priests and consistory members decorated with pectoral crosses that bore his own
name. The most extraordinary conception of ecclesiastical honors,
however, was that which Smohozhevs'kyi and Stanisław August
put before Pope Pius VI in 1784. The purpose was to "decorate
the meritorious Ruthenian secular clergy" and "to serve to excite
them ever more in the service of religion and in the commitment
to conserve and propagate the Holy Union." The metamorphosis
of the *asini* was quixotically envisioned in the foundation of an
honorary order of Uniate secular priests, the Cavaliers of the
Holy Union. A total of twenty-four such decorations were to be
divided among the dioceses, with the metropolitan ceremonially
dispatching the crosses and diplomas. The special obligation
of the "cavaliers" would be to serve in the parishes and teach

---

169 Korczok, *Griechisch-katholische Kirche*, 46.

170 Madey, *Kirche zwischen Ost und West*, 115; Likowski, *Geschichte des allmaeligen Verfalls*, 1:286.

171 Pelesz, *Geschichte der Union*, 2:572.

Christian doctrine.[172] The survival of the Uniate Church obviously depended upon the competency and fidelity of its parish priests, and they were to be elevated in ecclesiastical standards by the lure of attaining the already almost anachronistic emblems of the ancien régime. The asses would have to recognize themselves as cavaliers in order to appreciate their own identity as Uniates.

All by Themselves

Pelesh in the nineteenth century estimated that there were twelve million Uniates before the partitions of Poland. Likowski calculated that the Union lost to Orthodoxy "at least seven and maybe even eight million" between the first partition in 1772 and Catherine's death in 1796. "If God had lengthened her lifetime by another several years," wrote Likowski piously, "she would have probably rooted out the rest (about two million)." This would suggest a total of nine or ten million. However, Emanuel Rostworowski puts the entire pre-partition population of the Polish-Lithuanian Commonwealth at twelve million, while Gershon Hundert notes a possible range from twelve to fourteen million. Witold Kołbuk has plausibly estimated the total number of Uniates in the Commonwealth in 1772, on the eve of the first partition, at 4,600,000. Johannes Madey estimates that there were still 1,400,000 Uniates in the Russian Empire in 1804, after Paul had canceled Catherine's final assault. If one estimates that 1,800,000 Uniates were safe from Catherine in Galicia, then a plausible estimation of the net loss in the Uniate population in the age of the Polish partitions would be 1,400,000.[173]

---

172 Smogorzewski, *Epistolae*, 340–41.

173 Pelesz, *Geschichte der Union*, 2:583; Likowski, *Geschichte des allmaeligen Verfalls*, 1:282; Davies, *God's Playground*, 1:513; Madey, *Kirche zwischen Ost und West*, 107; Korczok, *Griechisch-katholische Kirche*, 10; Emanuel Rostworowski, "The Society and Civilization of the Age of Enlightenment," in Aleksander Gieysztor, ed., *History of Poland*, (Warsaw, 1979), 293; Witold Kołbuk,

One may attempt to interpret the changes of affiliation in this period by borrowing Smohozhevs´kyi's idea of "vacillation," which he used with reference to the clergy in 1773, and then later in 1785 to describe the general state of the Union in this period: "the Holy Union itself still vacillating (*vacillante*)."[174] The pressures applied by Russian Orthodoxy—from 1768 to 1775 in Ukraine at the time of the first partition, from 1779 to 1783 in Belarus during the Polatsk vacancy, and from 1793 to 1796 through the final partitions—were all closed intervals followed by periods of recovery and return to the Union. If losses were significantly balanced by returns, then the bottom line of statistical attrition was consistent with Uniate survival. Indeed, the inflation of numerical losses may have derived partly from the same Uniates leaving and rejoining the Union more than once. Furthermore, real losses may have reflected not only the success of Orthodox campaigning but also the weakness of Uniate identity and commitment. Bieńkowski has concluded that "the Union was often accepted by the parish clergy and the Ukrainian population only seemingly (*pozornie*), as revealed by events between 1768 and 1773, when a very significant number of parishes returned to Orthodoxy (in truth, partly under compulsion)."[175] Especially since Uniate proselytism continued strong through the first half of the eighteenth century, those "lost" in the second half may have been barely Uniate to begin with.

In fact, the quantitative evaluation of gains and losses in this period is probably less important than the qualitative changes that occurred in the Uniate millions. One may consider the relevance of Delumeau's sociological model of Counter-Reformation Christianization and Enlightenment de-Christianization as "two

---

Kościoły wschodnie w Rzeczypospolitej około 1772 roku (Lublin, 1998), 72–76; Gershon Hundert, *Jews in Poland-Lithuania in the Eighteenth Century: A Genealogy of Modernity* (Berkeley: University of California Press, 2004), 23–24.

174   Smogorzewski, *Epistolae*, 385.

175   Bieńkowski, "Organizacja Kościoła Wschodniego," 858–59.

intersecting curves" in eighteenth-century Europe: "the one expresses a qualitative religion, the other a quantitative adherence." Such adherence could be almost perfunctory, an automatic matter of default in the absence of other options, but by the eighteenth century this mere "conformism" was beginning to be challenged by the possibility of choice. In the religious sociology of Gabriel Le Bras, the whole notion of "de-Christianization" could be considered as a misconception for early modern populations—"since to be dechristianized they must at some stage have been christianized." By the same token, Uniate "apostasy" to Orthodoxy was an empty lament, if the alleged apostates had been only minimally aware of being Uniates.[176] Yet those who had been pressured to apostatize to Orthodoxy, or counseled to consider transit to Roman Catholicism, whether they stood fast or whether they succumbed and then returned, were not the same Uniates they had been before. The religious ebbing and flowing of this period dramatized for the Uniates an array of religious alternatives, and those who ultimately had to decide whether or not to sign on the line in 1794 were raised to a higher and more modern level of religious consciousness. Vacillation became the crucible of affiliation and identity.

The Union of Brest in 1596 was the work of the bishops. When they left Orthodoxy for Catholicism and rejected their ecclesiastical association with Moscow and Constantinople to submit themselves to the hierarchical authority of the pope in Rome, they theoretically brought their dioceses along with them. Because of the nature of the Uniate compromise—its preservation of the Greek rite and Slavonic liturgy—the reorientation of those bishops did not dramatically affect the millions subject to their pastoral care. Indeed, the Union was all the more of a coup for the fact that it converted those millions by a stroke of the pen, regardless of their agreement or even awareness. Perhaps not until the Synod of Zamość in 1720 did certain forms of liturgical

---

176   Delumeau, *Catholicism between Luther and Voltaire*, 213, 227.

Latinization make the union into something manifestly percep-
tible in the religious life of the ordinary churchgoer. Supposedly,
Uniates of the Commonwealth who lived near the border with the
Russian Empire were known to cross over on Sundays to attend
the gorgeous churches of Kyiv. Konys´kyi in 1773 would boast that
many Uniates remained Orthodox "in their hearts" and secretly
sneaked off to Orthodox churches, but it is just as likely that
they attached little importance to the difference between Uniate
and Orthodox churches with their similar services.[177] It became
much more obviously important after 1768, when those churches
began to change hands violently back and forth between Uniate
and Orthodox. At the same time, the Uniate Church became a
more meaningful concept to the millions who saw it challenged
from parish to parish, while those millions attracted the more
attentive interest of the Uniate hierarchy, which had to forestall
the seizure of its social base. Attention to the religious life of
parish priests and their parishioners, as sponsored elsewhere in
Europe by the Tridentine Counter-Reformation in the sixteenth
and seventeenth centuries, now at last became a serious issue
in the Uniate Church.

The struggle between the Basilian order and the parish priests
was more than just intraclerical combat, because the divisions of
the Uniate clergy reflected the tremendous distance and virtual
nonrelation between the episcopal apex and the peasant masses
at the top and bottom of the Uniate Church. The Latin-leaning
Basilians, ever since Zamość, were the elite pool from which
bishops were chosen, while the secular priests—working farms,
fulfilling feudal obligations, and supporting families—were cul-
turally and socioeconomically close to the peasant laity who
attended the parish churches. Those priests were often the sons
of priests, carrying on a vocation across the generations without
ever rising far above the level of the peasantry they attended.
The separation between elite and base was all the starker for the

---

177   Likowski, *Geschichte des allmaeligen Verfalls*, 164, 1:190.

fact that the Uniate nobility had largely disappeared in the seventeenth century, drawn by the elite attraction of Polish Roman Catholicism with or without the incitement of a Jesuit education; in the eighteenth century the Uniate laity was almost entirely of the peasant class, farming at the miserable level of serfdom in the Commonwealth. This social circumstance was expressed in the pejorative Polish proverb, "ruska wiara, chłopska wiara," equating "Ruthenian faith" to "peasant faith."[178] Therefore, when the bishops finally had to look to their base in the late eighteenth century, they had to search right down to the bottom of society. The only possible mediating order was that of the parish priests whose much-lamented "ignorance" was not without its advantages, for it signaled not only distance from elite piety but also proximity to popular culture. Uniate religious mobilization in this period became a point of departure for the later evolution of modern peasant national affiliation in Belarus and Ukraine. The Synod of Zamość prescribed the publication of a general catechism and a manual for the clergy in the vernacular language of the Ruthenians; the latter was printed at the Basilian monastery of Supraśl in 1722 as *Sobranie pripadkov kratkoe i duchovnym osobom potrebnoe.*[179]

According to Delumeau, the lower classes of Europe were discovered to be deeply superstitious, even pagan, in the seventeenth century—in Brittany, for instance, kneeling to the moon while reciting the Lord's Prayer—and therefore the task of the Counter-Reformation was no less than the thorough "Christianization" of society. Even in the eighteenth century, "it would certainly not be very difficult to gather numerous documents on the religious ignorance of the masses and the survival of superstition."[180] In Josephine Galicia, the Uniate bishops addressed themselves to this same problem in the 1780s, and their specific concerns gave some

---

178 Likowski, *Geschichte des allmaeligen Verfalls*, 1:296.

179 Senyk, "Education of the Secular Clergy," 410–11.

180 Delumeau, *Catholicism between Luther and Voltaire*, 161–62, 175, 225.

idea of eighteenth-century popular culture among the Uniates. Ryllo, bishop of Chełm, issued a pastoral letter in 1781, warning his diocese against celebrating unauthorized festivals, making religious use of images and herbs to heal the sick, throwing children before the feet of the priest at communion, believing in dreams for prophecy, fearing that extreme unction causes death, lighting candles in church with prayers for revenge, and involving poultry, cattle, and goats in various religious practices. Ryllo urged his clergy to remind the people that "not the saints, and much less their images, are capable of working wonders, but only God alone."[181] Historian Valerie Kivelson has studied the coexistence of magical practice and Orthodox religion in early modern Russia, and an analogous incongruity was clearly also to be found within the Uniate communities of the Commonwealth.[182]

Bilians'kyi, archbishop of Lviv, issued his own pastoral letter in 1788, specifically addressed to both clergy and laity: "To the secular and regular clergy as well as the people of the dioceses of Lviv, Halych, and Kam'ianets, regarding the elimination of several superstitious uses and abuses." These included putting little pictures or writings under the communion cup during mass, and relying on "prayers in a specific number, performed in a specific way and at a specific time"—but not, apparently, specified by the Church—to cure the ills of humans and cattle. Bilians'kyi was aware that "here and there are found springs and streams to which the people go in crowds, in the superstitious opinion that one could be freed of all sickness and unwellness by washing and submerging, if one left behind a piece of clothing." Similarly, there were known to be places where "so-called wonder-working images are found," and where "the people are accustomed to gather in great crowds, and worship and esteem these images so highly as to attribute to them even miraculous power." Such episcopal

---

181 Korczok, *Griechisch-katholische Kirche*, 20–23.

182 Valerie Kivelson, *Desperate Magic: The Moral Economy of Witchcraft in Seventeenth-Century Russia* (Ithaca: Cornell University Press, 2013), 52–82.

appeals signaled the sort of movement toward "Christianization" described by Delumeau, and also that religious "reform of popular culture" described by Peter Burke.[183]

Though these developments came to the Commonwealth along with the Roman Catholic Counter-Reformation, there was a particular reason for their long delay in reaching the Uniate Church. The Union compromise, as Smohozhevs´kyi explained it in St. Petersburg in 1773, allowed the Uniates to preserve their "sacred rites and truly pious and honest customs." His eighteenth-century qualification—"truly pious and honest"—matched the concerns of Ryllo and Bilians´kyi, but he dared not deny the association of rites and customs. The millions could acquiesce in the Union because, by preserving their rites and customs, it affected their religious life so little, but such a commitment to the cultural status quo made any challenge to popular culture both arguably illegitimate and dangerously provocative. Even in 1774, when Smohozhevs´kyi considered proposals for reducing the number of religious holidays, he was in no hurry to take advantage of selective reduction to reinforce the Catholicism of his Uniates. He thought it would be best to wait on the Orthodox Church, and match its reductions, for fear that otherwise "the Catholic peoples could reduce themselves to schism precisely because in the other church they were observing the festivals and being idle." The idleness of festival days reflected for the archbishop the religious passivity of people who consented to be Uniates as long as that did not upset their customs. The pun on "reduction" was his: by the "reduction" (*riduzione*) of holidays one risked provoking the people to "reduce themselves" (*ridursi*) to Orthodoxy. Burke, in his discussion of "the world of carnival," has suggested the importance of festival celebrations for popular culture in early modern Europe.[184]

---

183 Kivelson, *Desperate Magic*, 22–23; Peter Burke, *Popular Culture in Early Modern Europe* (New York, 1978), 207–43.

184 Smogorzewski, *Epistolae*, 116; Burke, *Popular Culture in Early Modern*

At the same time, indeed in the same dispatch of 1774, Smo-
hozhevs´kyi expressed his characteristically eighteenth-century
confidence that education—"instruction in the sciences"—was
the key to the Uniates' religious stability: "because deep down
(*in fondo*) they are optimal Catholics, and they will be so for certain
(*lo saranno per certo*)."[185] His confidence in the future, and in the
Uniate souls "deep down," rebutted Konys´kyi's backward-looking
insistence in 1773 that the Uniates remained Orthodox "in their
hearts." Whatever they had been in the past, Smohozhevs´kyi
accepted that education was the key to their future, and popular
"ignorance"—the guarantee of religious acquiescence in centuries
past—could no longer support the Union in the politically pressured age of the partitions. The most engaged analyst of this state
of affairs was Garampi at the Warsaw nunciature, from 1772 to
1776, observing the Orthodox occupation of Uniate churches in
Ukraine. "The people blindly follow their pastors," he wrote, "and
ignorance makes them blindly obey schismatic priests who intrude
themselves." Here "ignorance" was specifically identified as the
root of apostasy, though as Garampi might have pointed out as
well, that was how those same people had entered the Union to
begin with. His particularly condescending Italian Roman Catholic
perspective on Uniate ignorance was developed in his *Exposé of
the Condition of the Church in Ukraine* in 1773, aimed at arous-
ing the concern of the Polish Sejm. He warned that the Uniates
of the Commonwealth, once having apostatized to Orthodoxy,
would become virtually subjects of the Russian Empire: "Ignorant
and course, often rough men, sometimes superstitious, almost
always stupid—they are certainly incapable of distinguishing
civil from religious obedience." The conjunction of ignorance and
superstition on the one hand, and coarseness and roughness on
the other, neatly associated the dimensions of popular culture
and peasant society as something potentially subversive. The

Europe, 178–204.

185   Smogorzewski, *Epistolae*, 115.

dangers were spelled out in Garampi's 1774 proposal of an appeal to Constantinople, warning that the Russian government would use Orthodoxy to enslave and exploit the people of Ukraine, "a people capable of every transport and barbarism when one proposes to them a pretext or motive of supposed—and always misunderstood—religion."[186] Though "ignorance" was a catch-all concept, expressing the nuncio's Italian condescension, there was one fundamental issue at the center of his concerns: the understanding and misunderstanding of religion.

When the abolition of the Jesuits and their Jesuit schools led to the formation of the Polish National Education Commission in 1773, Garampi immediately envisioned new schools that might remedy "the extreme roughness and supine ignorance of the Ruthenian peoples." In 1774, while Smohozhevs´kyi was hopefully waiting for vacancies in the Pontifical College in Vilnius, Garampi was worrying about funding for that same institution which was said to provide "in the whole Ruthenian nation the only priests who are well instructed and qualified to instruct the people."[187] Thus, he clarified explicitly that the most fundamental reason for educating the ignorant parish priests was so that they could educate their ignorant parishioners. The same point was made by the first Habsburg governor in Galicia in 1773, remarking upon the "stupidity of these miserable people." They were ignorant of the "basic principles of religion," because of "lack of schools and lack of vigilance on the part of the clergy." Joseph in 1784 ordered the establishment of a school in every parish. Starting in 1787 every parish priest was required every year to deliver a special sermon urging attendance at school.[188] The convergence of political adaptations, religious imperatives, and enlightened

---

186   Wolff, "Vatican Diplomacy and the Uniates," 401, 406, 411; ANV 58, Garampi, 16 July 1774; ANV 59, Garampi, 15 March 1775.

187   Wolff, "Vatican Diplomacy and the Uniates," 400–1; ANV 58, Garampi, 19 January 1774 and 19 March 1774.

188   Korczok, *Griechisch-katholische Kirche*, 20, 32.

conventions made the dialectic of ignorance and education important throughout the partitioned Uniate domain.

In the Commonwealth in the early eighteenth century the founding of a church in the Polissia (Polesie) region occasioned the comment, in 1705, that the villagers scarcely considered themselves Christians, and some preserved the practice of ancient Lithuanian paganism; meanwhile, "the true Christians who find themselves in these villages leave this world without baptism, and without the holy sacraments of penance." In 1765 the founding of a parish church in the Ashmiany (Oszmiana) district near Vilnius was intended for communities that "having no definite parish, and separated by distance from other churches and parishes, often leave this world without proper knowledge of the rudiments of the holy faith and without the holy sacraments, except for holy baptism." In 1766 the magnate Franciszek Potocki established schools at Uman in Ukraine for peasants on the Potocki family estates, explaining that the schools were "not only intended for the education in piety and knowledge of the simple peasants, but also and above all for those who aspired to the clergy of the Greek rite."[189] Thus, on the eve of the religious crisis in Ukraine, about to erupt with the arrival of Russian troops in 1768, there was already awareness and concern about the religious ignorance of the Uniate population, which was clearly related to the scantness of the institutional infrastructure of priests, churches, and schools in the Commonwealth.

The pastoral visitations conducted in the 1780s in the diocese of Chełm revealed both the depth of the problem and a new level of commitment to undertaking the remedy. A series of catechistic questions to the faithful produced devastating results:

"What is the Trinity?" "The Mother of God."
"Who is Christ?" "The Holy Trinity."[190]

---

189 Bieńkowski, "Organizacja Kościoła Wschodniego," 976, 986–87.
190 Bieńkowski, "Organizacja Kościoła Wschodniego," 997.

The proffered explanation for such confusion was that the parish priest taught nothing to his parishioners. In 1783, when a visitation yielded analogous instances of ignorance in another parish, the priest was sent off for a four-week course in basic religion at the Chełm seminary. In 1787 pastoral visitors already noted a generation gap among the Uniates, inasmuch as "especially the younger parishioners know well the rudiments of faith, but older ones know less since the previous priests did not teach them." A Uniate catechism of 1792 addressed the always perplexing question "What is a Catholic?" and prescribed the answer: "A Catholic is an obedient child with the Catholic Church as Mother and the Pope as Father of all Christianity." The improvement of education among the Uniate clergy was correlated with a diminution of religious ignorance among the Uniate populations. Bieńkowski concludes that there was "significant progress" in the Christianization of the Uniates during the second half of the eighteenth century, though more in breadth than in depth, as basic religious knowledge was extended to a greater percentage of the Uniate population.[191]

A traveler in Galicia in 1800 noted that "the piety of the Ruthenian peasants rests more on form than on actual grasping and understanding of religious content."[192] Though "form" was generally important for early modern piety, providing the basis for what Delumeau notes as religious "conformism," the significance of "form" was all the more fundamental in the Uniate Church, the raison d'être of which was the conservation of ritual and custom. In fact, considering the mass response to religious pressure in the age of the Polish partitions, it appears that the Uniate millions, in spite of their repeatedly deplored "ignorance" and "roughness," were more committed to the Union than anyone expected. The first to be surprised was Giuseppe Garampi. He, who had trumpeted

---

191 Bieńkowski, "Organizacja Kościoła Wschodniego," 989, 996–97; Skinner, *Western Front*, 79–80.

192 Korczok, *Griechisch-katholische Kirche*, 20.

their supine ignorance and blind subservience, who promoted fantastic appeals on their supine behalf to foreign courts, could not help noting and reporting in 1775 that the apostates were returning to the Union: "The various populations all by themselves (*da se stesse*) are reuniting (*riunendosi*) with us and pleading for their former pastors." He went so far as to credit the Uniates with returning "spontaneously."[193] Garampi, who only the year before had asserted as an axiom that "the people blindly follow their pastors," now found that the religious impetus was coming from "the people" themselves: "pleading for their former pastors." This was the Uniate Church turned upside down. The Union created by bishops on the pastoral premise of passive populations, now found the millions actively, "spontaneously," restoring the Union in Ukraine "all by themselves." In employing the reflexive verb *reunirsi*—"reuniting themselves"—Garampi even suggested that the act of Union was being recreated, this time from the bottom instead of from the top.

The worst fears of the Roman Catholic nuncio were no more justified than the rosy hopes of the Orthodox bishop, Konys´kyi, who in 1773 reminded the Uniates that "their fathers and ancestors" were Orthodox and appealed to the Orthodoxy hidden "in their hearts." In fact, almost two hundred years after Brest, the Uniate Church had a history of its own, and most Uniates looked back to Uniate fathers and ancestors. What they held in their hearts was the traditional ritual and popular culture that had been conserved within the Union. Konys´kyi's protégé, Sadkovs´kyi, would make the same appeal in 1794—to "arise" and return to "the Orthodox confession that inspired your ancestors"—but with the passing of another generation the Uniates knew better how to respond to the Orthodox rhetoric of ancestors. Facing the conversion campaign of 1794, some Uniate villagers were supposed to have declared, "In the faith in which we were born, so will we

---

193   Wolff, "Vatican Diplomacy and the Uniates," 419; ANV 59, Garampi, 30 August 1775 and 15 November 1775.

die. As to what faith our grandfathers had, we do not know, but we will not break our own faith."[194]

The spontaneous returns to the Union of the 1770s partly foretold the returns of the late 1790s, once again as soon as the pressure was lifted. The historian might even look further forward, to the 1990s, and the tremendous resurgence of the Union in independent Ukraine, as modern religious identity asserted itself anew after the removal of Soviet constraints. The Vatican of the 1990s might well have observed, echoing Garampi across the centuries, that "the various populations all by themselves are reuniting with us," and, unlike Pius VI, Pope John Paul II had the opportunity to witness the fruits of that reunion in person during his visit to Ukraine in 2001.

Smohozhevs'kyi in 1774, observing Ukraine from Belarus, did express confidence in the "constancy of the Ukrainians" (*la costanza degl'Ukrainesi*), but he betrayed his uncertainty by going on to suggest that "in my opinion there would be more value in the efficacy of a petition from Vienna," not to mention the involvement of "other Catholic courts."[195] Faced with the episcopal impotence of himself and his fellow bishops, he was capable of looking to the local populations, but preferred, like Garampi, to appeal to the courts. His hopes of popular "constancy" were nevertheless insightful as well as predictive, for he seemed to appreciate the dialectic by which constancy could emerge from vacillation. His designation of the "Ukrainians" offered an eighteenth-century territorial usage of what would eventually become the nineteenth-century national name. This reference to the peasant population of Ukraine suggested the importance of early modern religious affiliation for the evolution of modern national identity. The Ukrainian national historian Mykhailo Hrushevs'kyi, who came from Orthodox Kyiv to Uniate Galicia in

---

194   Likowski, *Geschichte des allmaeligen Verfalls*, 1:190, 268; Skinner, *Western Front*, 214.

195   Smogorzewski, *Epistolae*, 120.

1894 to teach Ukrainian history at Lviv, argued that the Union had
originally been created by the Polish Commonwealth "to weaken
the national culture" of Ukraine. Yet ironically, as Hrushevsʹkyi
observed, "to the new generation which had been born into the
Uniate Church this faith was the national Ukrainian religion," and
as "the Church of the peasants" it became "a mirror of contemporary national life."[196] The Union, in protecting the rituals and
customs that constituted early modern popular culture, provided
in the late eighteenth century a base for the emergence of modern
religious and national identity in peasant society.

Such were the historical consequences of a religious union
that respected, as Smohozhevsʹkyi insisted it must, "the desires
of the nations" as expressed in "sacred rites and truly pious and
honest customs." It was the importance of those rites and customs
that undercut any easy assumptions about "blind obedience" on
the part of the peasant laity, just as it was Smohozhevsʹkyi's
strict interpretation of the union compromise that qualified his
own personal assurance of "blind obedience" to the Vatican in
1774. The "blindness" was perhaps exaggerated, literally as well
as figuratively, for only two months before he was awaiting "with
patience" in Polatsk the delivery of a pair of eyeglasses ordered
from Rome.[197] When Smohozhevsʹkyi was promoted to the metropolitanate in Poland in 1779, he left behind a budding crisis at
Polatsk, but arrived at his new post to find that the recent crisis
in Ukraine was basically over. The demonstrated vitality of the
Union there encouraged him to try to close the chasm that separated the Uniate hierarchy from its social base, and he planned
to divide his metropolitan activity between political business
in Warsaw and pastoral concerns in Ukraine with a residence
at Radomyshl:

---

196   Mykhailo Hrushevsky, *A History of Ukraine* (New Haven, 1941), 462,
469–70.

197   Smogorzewski, *Epistolae*, 145, 148.

> I have directed all my cares to the vast province of Ukraine, which
> is the largest portion of the metropolitanate. I have established
> myself in these parts, where until now no other metropolitan has
> ever made his residence, and I try, with my presence and my live
> voice (*colla viva voce*), to retain in the Holy Union those many
> populations, which after being seduced by the violence and fraud
> of the schismatics in the recent most unhappy turbulences of
> Ukraine, have in large number returned spontaneously (*spontanea-
> mente*) to the Catholic faith.[198]

His echoing of Garampi's word—"spontaneously"—confirmed the
verdict; a less strictly fair-minded prelate might have been tempted
to take more credit for himself in those returns to Catholicism.
Smohozhevs´kyi called it "the Catholic faith," of course, but no
one knew better than he how much and how little could be com-
prehended in "the perplexity of that one little word": Catholics.[199]

In the case of the Uniates of Ukraine, it was not necessary
for Smohozhevs´kyi to specify whether their return to the fold
was more a matter of Catholic faith or of customary culture. His
establishment of a residence in Ukraine adumbrated a new concern for pastoral proximity; the people had come seeking their
pastors, and the pastors would reciprocate with greater attention
to their flocks. Above all, it was the unexpected level of popular
attachment to the Union, as demonstrated in the "spontaneity" of
return from apostasy, that enabled the Uniate Church to survive
through the age of the Polish partitions. Those peasants who
"reunited themselves" were the unexpected actors in a modern
renewal of the Union, at a time when "the body of the Uniates"
was "split into so many completely different parts, and subject
to diverse heads."[200]

Alexander, John, *32*

---

198 Smogorzewski, *Epistolae*, 307.

199 Smogorzewski, *Epistolae*, 139.

200 Smogorzewski, *Epistolae*, 120.

Index